D0893292

Winning at Service

Lessons from Service Leaders

Waldemar Schmidt
Gordon Adler
Els van Weering

Other Wiley Editorial Offices

John Wiley & Sons Inc., 111 River Street, Hoboken, NJ 07030, USA

Jossey-Bass, 989 Market Street, San Francisco, CA 94103-1741, USA

Wiley-VCH Verlag GmbH, Boschstr. 12, D-69469 Weinheim, Germany

John Wiley & Sons Australia Ltd, 33 Park Road, Milton, Queensland 4064, Australia

John Wiley & Sons (Asia) Pte Ltd, 2 Clementi Loop #02-01, Jin Xing Distripark, Singapore
129809

John Wiley & Sons Canada Ltd, 22 Worcester Road, Etobicoke, Ontario, Canada M9W 1L1

Wiley also publishes its books in a variety of electronic formats. Some content that appears in
print may not be available in electronic books.

British Library Cataloguing in Publication Data

A catalogue record for this book is available from the British Library

ISBN 0-470-84823-5

Typeset by Dobbie Typesetting Ltd, Tavistock, Devon.
Printed and bound in Great Britain by T.J. International Ltd, Padstow, Cornwall.
This book is printed on acid-free paper responsibly manufactured from sustainable forestry
in which at least two trees are planted for each one used for paper production.

*To all the millions of service people who work
day-in day-out to improve the quality of our lives*

Contents

List of Contributors

Austin, Chantal, Regional Manager, Securitas AB
Bellon, Pierre, Chairman, Sodexho Alliance SA
Berglund, Thomas, CEO of Securitas Group and President of Securitas AB
Carton, Bernard, retired Vice President of Finance, Sodexho Alliance
Cuny, Jean-Pierre, Division Manager, Sodexho Alliance SA
Douce, Patrice, retired Chief Operating Officer, Sodexho Alliance SA
Dubois, Michel, retired Senior Vice President Strategy, Innovation and
    Quality, Sodexho Alliance SA
Dueholm, John, former COO of Group 4 Falck and as of 1 September 2002,
    Executive Vice President SAS, Scandinavian Airline Systems
Eikeland, Johnny, Information Officer and member of the board, Group 4
    Falck A/S
Grubbe, Bill, ex-Vice President Sales, Compass Group PLC
Holberg Fog, Tim, ex-Corporate Development Director, Compass Group
    PLC
Klein, Michael, CEO, Viterra Energy Services AG
Lawrence, Cathi, Corporate Communications Director, Compass Group
    PLC
Mackay, Francis H., Chairman, Compass Group PLC
Neubauer, Joe, Chairman and CEO, Aramark
Nørby Johansen, Lars, President and CEO, Group 4 Falck A/S
Petersen, Nels, Communications Director, Group 4 Falck A/S
Piponius, Kirsti, Managing Director, Sodexho Alliance SA

Pollard, Bill, Chairman, ServiceMaster

Ramsey, Bob, Head of Department, UNI, Union Network International

Rijnierse, Hans, Managing Director Food and Management Services The Netherlands and South Africa, Sodexho Alliance SA

Rylberg, Eric, CEO, ISS A/S

Sabatino, Tony, Area Manager, Securitas AB

Sand, Torben, Financial Analyst, Svenska Handelsbanken AB

Sharpe, Linda, Principal, Group 4 Falck Academy, Group 4 Falck A/S

Sørensen, Jorgen Philip, Chairman of the Board of Directors, Group 4 Falck A/S

Stern, Andrew, President, SEIU, Service Employees International Union

Stern, Erik, Managing Director, Stern Stewart Europe Ltd

Sutton, Richard, Group HR Director, Group 4 Falck A/S

Svanberg, Carl-Henric, President, Assa Abloy AB and CEO, Assa Abloy Group

Venneman, Anette, Head of Internal Affairs, Securitas AB

Foreword

Over the years, I've read my way around the libraries of management literature, and it seems to me that a large majority of management books are about Great American Companies. But *Winning at Service: Lessons from Service Leaders* is about four Great European Companies that have become world leaders in a very short time. In the security services industry, Securitas and Group 4 Falck are numbers one and two; Compass Group and Sodexho Alliance have reached the same rank in the food service industry. The four firms have more than one million people on their combined rosters. I'm an experienced service-industry CEO. I've been watching the four companies since they were small, and my admiration has grown right along with them. I've met with all the leaders of these companies individually many times to share experiences. We've met at investor seminars organized by institutional investors, who owned shares in our companies. Between us, we've traded non-core companies. Along the way, I've become a friend and dyed-in-the-wool admirer of these five gifted leaders: Pierre Bellon (Sodexho Alliance – from now on also referred to as 'Sodexho'), Thomas Berglund (Securitas), Francis Mackay (Compass Group – from now on referred to also as 'Compass'), Lars Nørby Johansen, CEO of Group 4 Falck and J. Philip-Sorensen, Founder of Group 4, now Chairman of Group 4 Falck, respectively. And now I've finally had the chance, with a great team, to show how these four stellar companies have managed to conquer the service world.

Our ambition in *Winning at Service* is to give managers in the service industry around the world the same opportunity I've had, namely to learn invaluable lessons directly from five leaders who have built world-class service companies from very humble beginnings.

Invited by Professor Peter Lorange, I came to one of the world's best business schools, IMD in Lausanne, Switzerland, as an Executive-in-Residence in the beginning of year 2000 to study some of the leaders I'd met during my nearly 30 years in the service industry. My idea was modest and, it seemed to me, pretty simple: I would write a business case study about leadership to be taught at IMD. I assembled a team to help me, and we quickly discovered that my subject – even if we zeroed in on the four companies only – was so rich that we could, instead, write a useful book. After I first talked with the five leaders, the project took yet another twist. They all agreed to take part! However, there was one condition: the book for which we now had such grandiose plans had to be about their companies, not about them as individuals. So we set out to describe how these four companies managed to become world leaders.

Back to my reading experience: I've found, over the years, that management books, though brilliant, are often complex, with long sentences and conceptual leanings and – let's just say – difficult reading for busy managers. I wanted *Winning at Service* to be a very easy read for busy executives. I tend to read management books as I read accounts: bottom line first, then top line. If this angle of attack gives me a clear picture, I stop. But if things are still unclear, I scour the accounts, in detail, hunting for answers to my questions. So busy reader, try the following. Read the 'Introduction', perhaps also 'The Journey to Leadership', which in early drafts we aptly named 'Key Everything', then read 'Winning at Service, Final Words'. These three chapters, like the rest of the chapters that form the book, are meant as stand-alones. Reading the 'top line' and the 'bottom line' of the book will give you a sense of our story. Then read the rest of the book, one chapter at a time, out of order, dipping, skimming, spotting useful passages. You'll find intriguing quotes from some of the people we interviewed, practical cases and examples and insights from the companies that have never before been published.

Do the four service companies offer lessons for managers outside the service industry? Indeed they do. Read our story about how Assa Abloy has become the world's largest lock manufacturer, and you will see that the lessons from our service companies have been successfully applied by its CEO Carl Henric Svanberg and his team. I'm convinced. I believe that managers in fragmented industries – no matter whether in service, retail or manufacturing – can learn some practical lessons from our four companies and their leaders. I would even dare say that if you share my conviction that 'people make the difference', you should be able to apply some of the lessons from the book. But whether you find one lesson or one hundred, it is, in my experience as a manager, not enough to read *Winning at Service* and then try the ideas out for a while. Becoming a great company, anywhere at any time, takes a great deal of stamina and will-power for ten, fifteen or even twenty years. Good luck!

Waldemar Schmidt
IMD, Lausanne, Switzerland
January 2003

Acknowledgements

In early 2001, Waldemar Schmidt came to IMD, the International Institute of Management Development, as Executive in Residence, with the idea of studying the leaders he had known during his three decades as a service industry executive and, perhaps, write a business case study about leadership for use at IMD. Over time, his first thoughts of doing business case studies gelled into a determination to write a book about four of the world's greatest service firms. Peter Lorange, President of IMD, showed a willingness to take a chance on Waldemar and the other two authors of this book. Thank you, Peter. And thanks to IMD for supporting us as we ran wild through the services industry.

High up on the list of people who made this book possible are the leaders of the four firms we wrote about – Pierre Bellon of Sodexho, Thomas Berglund of Securitas, Francis Mackay of Compass and Lars Nørby Johansen and J. Philip Sørensen of Group 4 Falck – who were also willing to take a chance, and who gave us the keys to their incredible kingdoms. A special thank you goes to staff at Securitas who allowed us to use pictures of the 'Securitas tools' that so aptly illustrate some of the lessons learned. Thank you, also, to the many employees and ex-employees of the four companies for vital information and unforgettable quotes. In this large group of dedicated employees a few stand out for repeatedly helping us make sense of the companies' stories: Anette Venneman, Michel Dubois and Nels Petersen. Industry experts like Bill Pollard, Chairman of ServiceMaster in the USA, union representatives like Andrew Stern,

President of SEIU in New York, USA, and Bob Ramsey, UNI (Union Network International) in Nyon, Switzerland, financial analysts like Torben Sand of Svenska Handelsbanken in Copenhagen, Denmark, and several investment bankers told us what they thought of the four companies, and although most of their names appear in small print with their quotes, we thank them again here.

Claus Colliander, of Egon Zehnder International, Copenhagen, and Peter Slagt, of McKinsey & Company, Brussels, gave more time than they could probably afford, and liberally shared their firms' resources. Thank you Claus and Peter for your invaluable ideas for the book, contacts for our research, and logistical help. Their colleagues, many of whom remained voices at the other end of the telephone and names on lists, analysed data and dug up diamonds of information we otherwise would never have found ourselves. A special hats-off goes to Per-Nicklas Höglund, McKinsey & Company, Stockholm. Time and again, Per-Nicklas earned our special gratitude and admiration for his vigilance, his insight, his stamina, his smarts and his commitment to finding time to read yet 'one more draft'. Thank you, Per-Nicklas, for helping us to appear better informed, more intelligent and certainly more 'logical' than we probably are. Where we look foolish, or make a poor argument or have our facts wrong, it's no one's fault but our own.

In the able-assistance department, key people from the five companies loom large: Josephine Bjorkman of Assa Abloy, Isabelle Honoré of Sodexho Alliance, Helen Karlsson of Securitas, Trisha Keaveny of Compass Group, and Dorthe Lundgaard-Jensen and Sue Teff of Group 4 Falck. They are joined by a legion of other company people whom we shy away from naming for fear of missing one out. Thanks go, as well, to our colleagues at IMD, who cheered us on, wised us up, lent an ear and helped us in so many ways. Thanks to John Evans, Manager of the IMD Information Center, and his confederates, especially Laure Meuret, for digging up even the rarest of company titbits. Thanks also to the people who transcribed our hundreds of minutes of taped interviews: Lindsay Baxter, Debbie Brunettin and Susanne Askov, who also assisted Waldemar Schmidt. Thanks to Claire Plimmer, Senior Publications Editor, and Sandra Heath, designer, and all the other people at Wiley & Sons who worked on this book.

Thanks to everyone else in the service industry who shared a shred of a tale, a fact, a statistic, an insight. Don't stop now: there's too much good in the services industry to end with this modest book.

Waldemar Schmidt
Gordon Adler
Els van Weering
IMD
Lausanne, Switzerland
January 2003

1

Introduction

In the twentieth century the service industry evolved from representing 10%–20% of the Western European economy (GDP) to being the heartbeat of the industrialized world. In economic importance, service industries have, by far, outgrown manufacturing, raw material extraction and agriculture. By the turn of the millennium the total services sector constituted approximately 65% of the total European Union (EU) GDP and 70% of the total workforce in the European Union. In this book we speak about a large but little publicized part of the services sector: companies that provide organizations and individuals with services such as food services and security service. Over the last century, most food services and security companies stayed small, or disappeared. But four European service companies – Securitas, Group 4 Falck, Compass Group, and Sodexho Alliance – grew on average at an aggregated rate of 25%, and overtopped all others, including their American counterparts. Stern Stewart Europe ranked them at the top for value-creation:

> Group 4 Falck, Securitas and Sodexho all did well in our national value-creation rankings for 2000, which ranked companies according to which ones created the most value for shareholders. Compass Group was not ranked by Stern Stewart for 2000 because of issues surrounding its merger with and subsequent de-merger from Granada.
>
> Erik Stern, Managing Director, Stern Stewart Europe

How do we characterize these four service winners? They're part of the outsourcing industry, including services like cleaning, recruitment, security and food services. The *Financial Times* lists them as 'support services' companies; the *Fortune 500* classifies them as diversified outsourcing companies. With humble starts in Sweden, Denmark, the United Kingdom, and France, these four grew into large, world-class companies. They have over the last 10–15 years generated remarkable long-term value for shareholders, on a par with or better than 'best in class' companies like Hennes&Mauritz, Wal-Mart, GE, Alcoa and other toppers. What's behind their exceptional and profitable growth?

In the last decades before the turn of the century, many companies prospered from the tremendous opportunities to create value in the service industry. Service companies make up about 70% of the firms that have generated the most shareholder value. They have rewarded their shareholders with value increases of thousands of percent. Over the last five years, many service indexes on the major European stock exchanges have outperformed other industry indexes. Nevertheless, despite the many service success stories, most *food service* and *security* companies failed to ride the upsurge in opportunity. And yet, Compass Group, Group 4 Falck, Securitas and Sodexho did.

You might think that a company managing world operations from the Old Continent would be at a serious disadvantage. The European labour market, unlike its American counterpart, is highly regulated by local legislation and EU directives, and suffused by strong unions. These challenges make the accomplishments of the four service winners all the more noteworthy, for they have managed to turn the European labour market hurdles into building blocks rather than road blocks. How? They spun value from simple credos, among them: you must, on threat of failure, treat your employees and customers with respect; you must never compromise quality of service for short-term monetary gain.

Somehow, these four untouted service companies made much more of unprecedented growth opportunities. Between 1980 and 2002, each of the four surged into higher gear: up went turnover, profit, number of employees and number of countries with operations. They changed into global heavy hitters that – all four combined – operate in more than 90 countries, with a total of more than one million employees and millions of customers. They hold global first and second in their industries: security and food services. They sell services worth about €35 billion per year and, at the end of October

2002, had a combined market value of more than €21 billion. Global institutional investors, including American ones, invest substantial sums in all four. Financial analysts have high expectations for their continued growth. Nevertheless, with the dramatic downturn on all stock exchanges in 2001 and 2002 it is relevant to ask if the shareholder value that outstripped peers and indexes in the 1990s has been significantly eroded. The answer: the 2001/2002 market valuation blindsided our companies, too. But the large drop in their share prices has been on par with peers and indexes. Despite the recent downturn, over five to ten years, the four have still on average, produced returns to their shareholders of several hundred percent.

Pure luck, you say. These four companies could only thrive in low-prestige, labour-intensive businesses where many of their competitors are notorious for shady business ethics, such as keeping wages low or not paying all employee hours. Wrong. We looked at one small Nordic lock manufacturer, Assa Abloy, that was once two separate Nordic companies, Assa and Abloy, that merged and, in a few short years became the world's largest and most accomplished lock-maker. How? Assa brought off the same feat by following, to a large extent, the Securitas path. The CEO had been a Securitas manager, and cut his milk teeth on the guarding services business model and philosophy. Assa's achievement suggests that our four companies didn't win on luck alone: their tools, methods and philosophies may be useful for managing in other industries such as manufacturing and perhaps even in the public sector.

In short, the success of these four companies is a story of their unique strengths, a story with potent human resources, operations and strategy themes. How can we explain it? For one, service industries are generally low-profile, labour-intensive – with up to 100% employee turnover per year – and have low barriers to entry. Service companies generally employ part-time, unskilled local labour. They don't peddle products, they sell services. Most of the time, Compass Group, Group 4 Falck, Securitas and Sodexho sites are working on mundane stuff. They provide guarding. They monitor burglar and fire alarms. They offer and run electronic surveillance systems. They service ATMs, count money, transport your cash and run prisons. They feed people at work, hospital patients and their visitors, and offer fast food, good food and fine drinks. In other words, as Sodexho describes its reason for being: they 'improve the quality of daily life for all'.

Our four companies depend on hundreds of thousands of employees scattered around the world at thousands of sites. Of all things, the success of these four companies comes down to people.

But there's more. Their achievements are inextricably linked, not just to people in general, but to long-standing leaders: Pierre Bellon (Chairman, Sodexho), Thomas Berglund (CEO, Securitas), Francis Mackay (Chairman, Compass Group), Lars Nørby Johansen (CEO, Group 4 Falck) and J. Philip Sørensen (Chairman, Group 4 Falck). Absent these leaders, the four service companies would likely have fallen short of today's results. Admittedly, no one man makes a world class company: more than anything, these five have led great teams. Nevertheless, they have been running 'their' companies for an average of 20 years each. Recall that eight out of 10 companies worldwide changed their top leader at least once during the 1990s, and in the last five years close to two-thirds of all major companies replaced their CEO.[1] So these twenty average year tenures alone set Bellon, Berglund, Mackay, Nørby Johansen and Sørensen apart. More than their tenures, however, it is style, character, knowledge and skill that set them apart. They are mild-mannered, yet powerful, visionary folk who achieve through simplicity and clarity, courage, knowledge, level-headed management and perception; in short, by following a quiet, no-nonsense approach of *just getting on with it*. They have a profound, holistic knowledge of and a clearly-defined vision for the business and the industry, a shared management philosophy based on care and respect for people at all levels. Effective leaders make a difference, and so do effective managers farther down the organization, but make no mistake: in this case, company accomplishment seems to spring, not from shining, larger-than-life evangelical characters so common to leadership literature, but from long-term, humble commitment.

Between 1980 and 2002, we learned, the four companies beat their competition with focus, passion for people, simplicity, long seniority among their top teams, and in-depth knowledge of the industry deeply ingrained in the fibre of the organization from the man at the top and right on out to the last person at the most remote site. And, the five leaders themselves noted,

---

[1] Cambron, Larry. 'The CEO's revolving door', *Far Eastern Economic Review*, 24 January 2002, p. 64.

some measure of luck. The paradox of our discovery is this: the growth of the four companies looks so simple and, in retrospect, obvious, that you might conclude any company could have pulled it off. Not so. Only these four did. What was their secret?

The investigation

We turned first to the business models the leaders described. We then spoke to the leaders, employees, industry experts, competitors, union leaders, financial analysts and customers, and studied data bases and annual reports. We asked: How have Compass Group, Group 4 Falck, Securitas and Sodexho become world leaders in their industries? We looked for common patterns in applied strategy across the four companies. Did the companies share certain organizational structures? We plumbed their operational models and processes. We asked if they shared or 'lived out' certain values. We hunted for unique tools in the companies' 'management tool boxes' (Securitas, it turns out, has a real wooden 'toolbox' for its 2000 branch managers) and asked how these tools contribute to company profit. Then we pondered: Does the successful business model of the four companies work in another industry?

The research

We grew familiar with the extensive literature and research on these companies and their industries, and considered any material in the public domain published in the last 10 years. But, this is not a theoretical book. It is in no way prescriptive, but rather descriptive. We relied on Waldemar Schmidt's service industry and business expertise. We lay no claims to profound scholarly knowledge or deep, wide academic experience or familiarity. We drew from facts and statistics provided by the IMD (International Institute for Management Development, Lausanne, Switzerland) Information Center, the companies themselves, Egon Zehnder International, in Copenhagen, Denmark, McKinsey & Company's European Service Strategy and Operations Practice based in Brussels, Belgium and Stockholm, Sweden, various data bases like Reuters

Business Briefing, Business Source Premier, and ProQuest, International press like the *Financial Times*, trade press like *Food Management* and the expertise of IMD colleagues. Our findings are further supported by third-party interviews and research conducted across various industries. But gathering exhaustive, incontrovertible data wasn't our aim. We wanted to shed light on four great service providers to reveal what distinguishes them from their more run-of-the-mill peers. And to share what they've done well, so that you, too, might benefit from their experience and success.

The interviews

The findings in this book are largely based on in-depth interviews with employees at all levels of the companies, from the people at the helm, including the CEO and/or Chairman of the Board, to the people at the front line. We started with a set list of interview questions, but we let our interview partners take us wherever their comments led. At times, we followed digressions that strayed from our questions, but seemed to be leading to an important insight or experience (the questions we asked are shown in the Appendix). The interviews covered a wide range of subjects. We called on members of the four companies to share with us the awesome challenges they faced, their gains and losses, explanations for their success and personal management approaches. So this book is, in large measure, about listening to five top-notch leaders and members of their extensive teams talk about their companies. It is about sharing stories. Imagine, if you will, meeting our five leaders and members of their long-tenured teams and asking them how they ran the show. Imagine an extended conversation with each (something they otherwise rarely do), chats in their company corridors with staff, and interviews with financial analysts, key union leaders and peers.

The framework

During the interviews, research done and discussions among the members of the book team we developed a framework that describes how these companies excelled. Here are the basics:

1. Pick Your Game and Play It
2. Leadership At the Heart
3. Passion for People
4. Keep It Simple

Let's consider this framework in some depth. The four companies have, at critical junctures, decided what they needed to do to succeed, what they wanted to do, and stuck to it. Regardless of setbacks and challenges. Hence: **Pick Your Game and Play It**. In the last 10–20 years, they have developed and applied, in every part of their widely distributed networks, a *replicable business model*. To guarantee compliance to the extent needed, each *applies transparent and relatively simple performance measurement systems*.

The four companies have all had one *leader at the heart* since the onset of their strong growth. These five men have been trying to reshape their industries for decades – each is a *visionary industry shaper*. Passionate and inspirational, they lead teams of other leaders, who are equally inspired and passionate about the company and the industry. Our five care deeply for their people, and believe that one of the best ways to lead is to set the example for their employees and live out the company values whenever they can. They've been working in their industries and their particular businesses for decades, and so they have, not surprisingly, *an intimate business knowledge* and seem to play all the roles required of a CEO with ease. By **Leadership at the Heart**, we also mean leadership *from* the heart, for Bellon, Berglund, Mackay, Nørby Johansen and Sørensen are working with teams of managers and employees who model heartfelt, value-oriented leadership.

Winning at service is about winning with people, and our four companies have a **Passion for People**. They face startlingly high rates of employee turnover, and out of this need have found ways to effectively *recruit and integrate*, *develop*, and *retain* staff. But they also look beyond the company walls, developing partnerships with unions and works councils so they can increase the standard pay in their industries and add respectability to their professions.

To put into practice their passion for people, vesting them with responsibility and independence, the four companies maintain flat, decentralized organizations, with small head offices and relatively few hierarchical layers between the employee on the street or in the restaurant and the top management team. In order to let the people at the front line make decisions and to allow for diverse practices in each of their many local companies – for this is the only way to win at labour-intensive services – they strip their bureaucracies down to the bones and streamline their internal processes. They **Keep It Simple**.

How this book is organized

Chapter 2 is a sort of 'key everything' basket with snapshots of the companies, short histories of their 'journeys to leadership', the special service challenges they face, a look at the growth they've generated, and the lessons learned. The rest of the book devotes a chapter to each of the four main findings of our research, with more detail and qualitative evidence. The final chapter, a wrap-up and brief retrospective, describes the most important challenges any service organization faces in its 'journey to success', looks briefly at how Assa Abloy applied many of the tools and ideas in the book to win in the lock industry, and ends with some provocative questions about the potential for further growth of our four companies.

You can learn from the stories of Compass Group, Group 4 Falck, Securitas and Sodexho. But *Winning at Service: Lessons from Service Leaders* is anything but a quick-fix book. And it is decidedly not a dump of quantitative data. It is a simple guide with practical insights and stimulating thoughts that can help others succeed in service. The concepts are straightforward enough for any manager to use, and the language and presentation, we hope, will make for an easy read. In the spirit of simplicity we picked up from the four companies, we offer plain lessons, not easy tricks. As our four companies illustrate, excelling at service is about sticking to the 'secrets' for 5, 10, 15 or 20 years. If there is one lesson the hundreds of thousands of people in these four companies can teach us, it is this: the way is the goal. *Winning at Service* offers not a destination, but a journey.

2

The journey to leadership

The challenge

Our company has to satisfy three parties with different needs: the client, who wants the best possible price and the highest possible level of quality; our employees, who want the best salaries and maximum attention; and third, the shareholders who want to see their shares go up and who want maximum dividend. The only way to satisfy those three stakeholders is to grow.

Pierre Bellon, Chairman, Sodexho Alliance

Trace the sales growth curves of Compass Group, Group 4 Falck, Securitas and Sodexho between 1987 and 2002 (see Figure 2.1), and you see them jetting upward faster than all but a handful of their competitors (some of whom our companies have now acquired!) (see Figure 2.2). What you don't see in the rising curves are the knotty challenges the companies face as they ascend. What you don't see are the singular difficulties in a service business of holding four large, powerful sets of demands in equilibrium: employees, customers, investors and social groups. What are these challenges?

The four companies operate in ample, widely distributed networks: Compass Group boasts 360 000 employees in more than 90 countries; Sodexho 314 000 in 72 countries; Securitas 230 000 in 30; and Group 4 Falck 215 000 in more than 80. Try keeping all these individual service employees happy in a historically low-wage and low-prestige industry. The employees of the two contract caterers meet customers eye-to-eye at more than 70 000 restaurant sites in total. The employees in safety and security

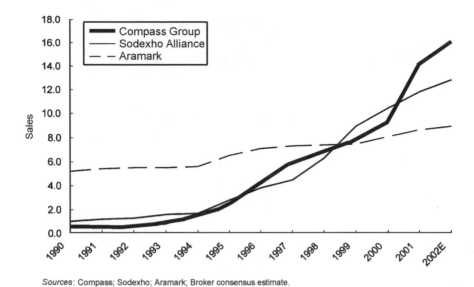

Sources: Compass; Sodexho; Aramark; Broker consensus estimate.

Figure 2.1 Sales development – food service companies (1990–2002E) (€ billions)

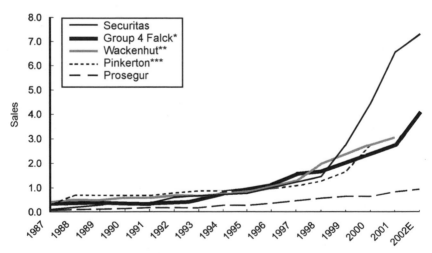

*Based on total sales of Group 4 and Falck before merger.
**Has been acquired by Group 4 Falck in 2002.
***Pinkerton acquired by Securitas in 1999.
Sources: Securitas; Prosegur; Group 4 Falck; Falck; Group 4; Pinkerton; Wackenhut, Broker consensus estimate.

Figure 2.2 Sales development – security companies (1987–2002E) (€ billions)

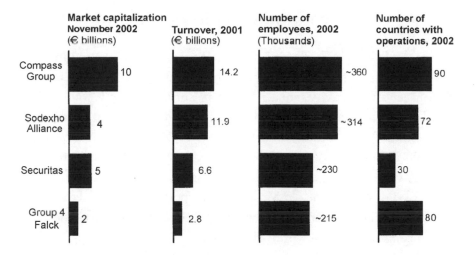

Sources: Thomson data stream; Hoover's; annual reports; web pages, interviews.

Figure 2.3 Case companies – overview

meet customers at even more sites. Choosy clients, who have a wide variety
of choice, from small, to medium, to large competitors, expect a lot in food
and security services. In every market, our four companies go up against
family operations that offer the customer a personal service that's hard to
compete with. They battle players who can trump them on price, if not
quality. With this stiff price competition, our companies not only have to
serve their customers well, they have to educate them to the necessity of
paying a fair price for their better, albeit 'intangible' services. To keep
institutional and private investors happy, our four companies have to
provide both short-term gains and long-term growth. At the same time,
they have to deal with demands from employees who want decent jobs with
fair pay. Unlike their American counterparts, who, except for sporadic
forays into Europe and Asia, have stayed pretty much in the American
market for services, the world's largest, most homogeneous, and most
focused on price, our four have had to cope with EU directives, navigate
Europe's highly fragmented and individually regulated markets, grapple
with powerful unions, co-determination and rigid labour laws. To better
understand how these companies profitably balance a cacophony of
competing requirements, let's take a look at the key events in their
journeys to the top (cf. Figure 2.3).

Four journeys to leadership

Securitas and Group 4 Falck sprouted from the same seed, planted in 1901, of a tiny guarding company across the street from Tivoli Gardens, Copenhagen's fun park. Compass Group began as Factory Canteens Ltd, started after a law passed in 1941 by the British Government that people working from 9 to 5 in munitions factories should have one hot meal per day. And Sodexho was started by one pioneer who had one hundred thousand French francs start capital and spent his days in a mini-van driving food to ships in the old Mediterranean port of Marseille. From these nondescript origins sprang the four most successful security and food services companies in the world. How is this?

By what paths and with what means did Compass Group, Group 4 Falck, Securitas and Sodexho become leaders in their industries? A close look at the journeys of our companies reveals that although the details and events on the five timelines differ, the *journeys* have many similarities:

1. Humble Beginnings and an Ordinary Life
2. The Turning Point
3. Pick Your Game
4. Internationalization
5. Industry Shaping Acquisitions

The Securitas journey to leadership

Humble beginnings and an ordinary life (1934–1985)

The humble beginnings of Securitas go back to 1934, when Philip Sørensen (grandfather of J. Philip Sørensen, Chairman of today's Group 4 Falck), the managing director of Denmark's largest security company De Forenende Vagtselskaber (The United Guard Company), opened a branch office in Helsingborg, Sweden, just across the Oresund from Hamlet's Castle in Elsinore, Denmark. During the next 50 years the company grew organically and by acquisitions to become Sweden's largest security company under the name of Securitas. In 1949 the business expanded into alarms, and also abroad. The company expanded into Norway, where it also became the market leader under the Securitas name. Philip Sørensen's son, Erik Philip-Sørensen was the Managing Director during much of this period. Erik's two sons, Sven and Jørgen Philip-Sørensen followed in the footsteps of their father and grandfather. Sven stayed in Scandinavia. Jørgen went abroad and started Group 4. Erik Philip-Sørensen eventually sold his business to his two sons. Sven bought the Swedish business which later became the foundation of the world's largest security company, Securitas. Jørgen bought the non-Swedish businesses, which he developed and in 2000 merged with Falck of Denmark under the name of Group 4 Falck, the world's second largest security company. Thomas Berglund, today's President of Securitas AB and CEO of the Securitas Group, joined the company in 1984 as a financial manager in one of the regions of the Swedish business. He was one of the 18 new managers hired during a period he describes as 'confused...not one of us knew anything about security, we were more or less preoccupied trying to go into one type of service or another'.

The turning point (1985)

In 1985 the company changed hands for about €20 million. Securitas was, at this time, a sagging firm: 5000 employees, with a little less than €100 million in revenues and €2–3 million yearly losses. It was acquired by a group of Swedish investors led by Gustaf Douglas who brought in Melker Schörling as the CEO.

Pick your game (1984–1989)

The new management of Securitas spent a lot of time trying to understand the business: the market, the customers, and what to offer the different customers. Despite the fact that all around Securitas competitors were still broadening their portfolios with other areas, management decided to abandon the idea of building a total service firm. The new Securitas team settled on a radical new direction. They would go the other way: focus solely on security services. As a consequence of this decision, which Berglund describes as 'the most important in company history', Securitas would carefully dispose, step-by-step, of all non-security services. Assa, the lock manufacturing division, was merged with the Finnish competitor Abloy. The merged company, Assa Abloy, was then spun off to Securitas' shareholders. Later, in 1996, Securitas would dispose of its alarm business for the elderly (Telelarm Care) and later of its contract cleaning activities. (As of 2002, Assa Abloy had become the world's largest lock manufacturer, with Carl-Henrik Svanberg as CEO. Svanberg had been an executive at Securitas since the mid-1980s.)

In parallel with restructuring its portfolio, Securitas management started to outline, formally, the core elements in their way of running the reshaped business. When it came to strategy, the fresh management wanted first to get things right in Sweden, build a rock-solid, local (i.e. country) organization, before they ventured out.

Internationalization (1989–1995)

For Securitas, the company's incursions abroad were cautious; in the CEO's words, 'the riskiest acquisition of all'. These first steps beyond Sweden's borders in 1989 were tentative, but they were, nevertheless, by virtue of the company's 50-year devotion to Sweden, a significant risk. Risk or not, the company bought the security operations of Group 4 in a number of countries all at once – Portugal, Norway and Denmark.

> *We started acquiring companies in other countries as we realized they had the same problems we had had: lack of focus.*
> *Thomas Berglund, CEO, Securitas*

The buying spree served as the acid test of the successful Swedish business model. Berglund had become Executive Vice President in 1988. The company's IPO came to fruition in 1991; three thousand of the five thousand eligible employees bought shares at market price and, over time, made a lot of money. A year later, it acquired a Spanish company (Esabe) and a French company Protectas (owned by the Swiss employment group Adia, now Adecco), with operations in France, Germany, Austria and Switzerland. In 1993 Berglund became President and CEO, and his predecessor, Melker Schörling, became non-executive chairman. In 10 years, Securitas had become the European market leader, number one in several European countries.

Berglund seemed like just the right man to lead a company out of some heavy turbulence. According to a recruiting consultant who has worked with Berglund for some time, Berglund is enormously focused, but never for his own gain. She describes Berglund as 'down-to-earth, not pretentious. He is hands on, analytical, systematic and thorough. And ... he always has time for people'.

Industry shaping growth (1995–present)

In the mid-1990s, its *accelerating growth* phase, Securitas really started to gain a seemingly unstoppable momentum, with strong organic growth going hand-in-hand with major strategic acquisitions. The company snapped up Raab Karcher Sicherheit from Veba (now known as Eon), Germany's largest power generating and energy conglomerate that comprised 125 businesses in Germany, Austria and the ex-Eastern block. A second large acquisition was Proteg from the French Ecco group, which is now part of Adecco, the employment company. The undisputed number one in Europe, Securitas, turned its sights on the United States, where, in February 1999, it paid US$390 million cash for the number two US security firm, Pinkerton. One year later, after several local acquisitions, another US$450 million bundle of cash bought America's biggest security firm, Burns. And a further US$175 million netted five more regional players across the country. By now, Securitas had roped in 20% of the US market, becoming the undisputed market leader.

With €6.6 billion in sales for 2001 and some 230 000 employees, Securitas had, in just over a decade, systematically made itself over: from domestic security business to Europe's leading security group to the world's number one. Together with Group 4 Falck it created a profession

Table 2.1 Key events in Securitas' history

1934	Founded in Sweden
1985	New owner and management; concentration in security
1988	Acquisition of Assa, Finnish lock maker. Established in Hungary
1989	Acquisitions in Norway, Denmark, Portugal
1991	Listing on Stockholm Stock Exchange
1992/93	Acquisitions in France, Switzerland, Spain, Austria, Germany, Finland
1994	Assa Abloy spun off to shareholders; 1st program of convertible shares offered to all employees
1996–98	Acquisitions in UK, Germany, Poland, Estonia, France, Sweden
1999	Acquisition of Pinkerton, USA
2000	Acquisition of Burns, USA, and further acquisitions in The Netherlands and Belgium
2001	Reorganization into four business areas and six divisions

and shaped the security industry. To meet rising demand after the 11 September 2001 terrorist attacks in the United States, Securitas trained and deployed an additional 10 000 guards (more than the total guards employed by the ninth and tenth largest US security firms combined and more than its total work force 15 years earlier). In the late 1990s and early 2000s, the company reorganized from a geographical structure to a regional organization covering four business segments: guarding, alarms, Securitas Direct (residential alarms) and cash-in-transit (CIT). To build market leading positions (which earlier existed only for guarding), it increased its focus on alarms and cash handling. As of 2002, its main business activities are security services (including guarding), security systems (including alarms), cash handling and direct (including home alarms).

Most recently, Securitas seems to be trying to *refocus even further*. The company keeps spinning off businesses and giving them to their shareholders to keep the company focused. It peels off layers of 'non-core' businesses to get, by iterations, nearer its 'core' business. This should not be a surprise since, if you ask around the security and contract management industries, you'll hear a common refrain: the more you focus, the more you learn; the better you understand the business, the sharper your eye for opportunity, the better your branding and positioning, the better organic growth and profitability.

The key events in Securitas' history are given in Table 2.1.

Group 4 Falck's journey to leadership

Humble beginnings and an ordinary life (1906–1983)

This is the story of two security companies – Falck and Group 4 – that lived two quite different and fairly ordinary lives during most of the twentieth century, but merged in 2000. The story of Falck begins in 1906, when Sophus Falck started The Rescue Company for Copenhagen and Frederiksberg, a rescue company (ambulance and fire brigade services). Falck gained national coverage in Denmark in the 1930s. It acquired its only large competitor, Zonen Redningskorps, in 1963. With Falck stations in every town in Denmark, Falck became a household name in Denmark. It had the image of a public service company – Falckmen were seen as really helpful. Already in the 1960s, 100 000 families had – and still have – subscriptions with Falck. The company covered a range of services: breakdown services for cars; house repairs in the case of storm damage to the roof or cellar flooding after torrential rain. As a service to its many subscribers who went on holiday by car to Germany and beyond, Falck set up a hotel and rescue station in Hamburg, Germany. However, in 1988, the Falck family decided to sell their company.

Group 4, started in 1962, was the brainchild of J. Philip-Sørensen, who, 38 years later, in 2000, became the Chairman of Group 4 Falck when his company merged with Falck. Sørensen is the grandson of Philip Sørensen, who founded Securitas in Helsingborg, Sweden, in 1934. Sørensen's 1962 beginning with Group 4 is a classic tale of entrepreneurship. His father sent him to Belgium with £50 000 to set up a guarding company. With no Flemish or French language skills and no customers, he found himself playing guard, salesman and general manager. Sørensen developed Group 4 in a very personal and entrepreneurial manner.

In 1964, his father sent him to England, where he managed a security company with 140 employees. Sørensen's business grew entirely by opportunistic organic growth. And, since then, strong organic growth has marked the way forward. Group 4's growth strategy was essentially to go into new markets, new countries with weak competition, and then grow organically. There were, however, a few acquisitions: in Austria (market leader) and Belgium (market leader). From the start, Sørensen showed that he could be very innovative with new services in more developed markets, such as winning contracts to build and operate prisons and emigration centres in the United Kingdom.

From its inception in 1962 until the merger with Falck in 2000, Group 4 grew with a constant energy. The real journey to leadership, however, is better seen through the eyes of Falck, which exhibited a clearly delineated turning point, focus, internationalization and then, once it merged with Group 4, the industry shaping acquisitions that have made the combined company, Group 4 Falck, the top service contender it is today.

The turning point (1988)

In 1988 the Falck family sold their company to a Danish insurance company, Baltica, that appointed Lars Nørby Johansen CEO of Falck. One financial analyst described Nørby Johansen as a man who 'fills the room with positive energy. He has always had great confidence in the potential of Falck and now Group 4 Falck and knew how to enthuse the market too!' Nørby Johansen himself says that this enthusiasm is sometimes a weak point: 'I am often too optimistic, too impatient, even after having been in the business for more than 15 years!'

His mission was to develop Falck into a safety and security company by building on Falck's unique public service image and culture. In 1988 Falck employed 7500 people and had annual sales of Da. Kr. 1760 million. It was a strong local Danish company with no international operations.

Pick your game (1988–1995)

The initial vision of Falck's new owners was to offer a 'safety package' that included insurance cover, the Falck services and security services (alarms) to private homes, the public sector and to business, initially in Denmark and then in the other Nordic countries. Over this seven-year period, the business vision evolved. The insurance company that owned Falck got into financial trouble and had to rethink its diversification strategy. Falck acquired some small alarm companies and became, after Securitas (called Dansikring in Denmark), the third largest player in Denmark. The market leader was ISS Securitas (established in 1901 and for many years managed by Philip Sørensen, grandfather of Group 4 Falck's current chairman). Nørby Johansen and his team gradually clarified and focused on what they wanted to do; more specifically, they spent a great deal of time defining and implementing a business concept that would be their springboard for internationalization. This process of defining and redefining created their vision of becoming a global player in the security industry, and a leading player in the safety and security business in the Nordic and Baltic Regions.

But, in order to have a platform for its international ambition in security services, Falck needed to acquire ISS Securitas in Denmark. This became possible in 1993 when ISS wanted to dispose of the company as part of its refocusing plans. Both Securitas and Falck bid for the business. Falck won the bid and got the much needed home base without which it might not have been able to build the strong global position it enjoys today. Falck also needed funds for its international ambitions. Access to funds was secured in 1995 when Falck was listed on the Copenhagen Stock Exchange.

Internationalization (1995–2000)

Now ready to start its international expansion, Falck went shopping. First in the Nordic countries, where it bought Partena Security from Sodexho in 1996 to become the second largest player in Securitas' home market, Sweden, and then the number two players in Norway and Finland. Falck went on to acquire security companies in the Baltic States, Germany and The Netherlands. And so it was that by the beginning of 2000 Falck had burgeoned into Europe's second largest security group, with a resilient safety business in the Nordic countries and Baltic States. Falck's annual turnover was Da. Kr. 7.2 billion, with 31 000 employees working in nine countries. It was ready for a quantum leap.

Industry shaping acquisitions (2000–present)

In May 2000 Falck and Group 4 announced their merger plans. Thus began the combined company's period of accelerated growth. Both Sørensen, the founder of Group 4, and Nørby Johansen, the CEO of Falck, had realized some time before that to seriously challenge Securitas, they needed both heft and clout:

> *With all the recent mergers in the industry, it was just too complex. If you wanted to be at the top, to play in the Champions' League, you just had to merge with another large company.*
> J. Philip-Sørensen, Chairman of the Board of Directors, Group 4 Falck

Both firms saw the need for being big and global and very strong financially. Both needed to jump into the higher orbits of global security services. The only way was to merge with another large company. In summer 2000, they signed their 'nuptial agreement'. The idea was to create a global player that could provide high-quality security and safety services to customers around the world. Wherever these customers might be, whether in the United States or Kazakhstan or Denmark or Bangladesh. The twinning of these two companies appeared, according to BNP Paribas Equities, 'to be a textbook example of a successful merger'. The Group's three core competencies would be security services, safety services and correction services, with contributions to revenue of 60%, 20% and 10% (another 10% consisted of miscellaneous other services). In 2001 the merged Group 4 Falck reached annualized turnover of €2.8 billion and a workforce of more than 148 000 operating in more than 50 countries. A very credible number two in the industry.

During the two years from 2000 to 2002, the new group, which had merged with few redundancies, melded into one group and acquired many

Table 2.2 Key events in Group 4 Falck history

1901	Philip Sørensen founds Kjøbenhavn Frederiksberg Nattevagt
1906	Sophus Falck founds Redningskorpset for København og Frederiksberg A/S
1930	Falck becomes nationwide operator
1934	Philip-Sørensen family established a new subsidiary in Sweden under the name of Securitas AB
1950	Philip-Sørensen family establishes its first company in the United Kingdom and takes over several small security businesses
1962	J. Philip-Sørensen starts Group 4 in Belgium
1963	The Philip-Sørensen family expands in United Kingdom. Falck buys Zonen Redningskorps
1988	Falck is sold to Baltica, a Danish insurance firm
1989	Group 4 moves into India
1991	Group 4 acquires Belgian firm, moves into Turkey
1993	Group 4 acquires firms in Austria and Canada
1994	Group 4 establishes operations in the United Kingdom and Ukraine
1992/93	Group 4 acquires US firm, moves into Hungary Falck acquires ISS Securitas, Denmark
1995	Falck listed on Copenhagen Stock Exchange
1996–99	Falck acquisitions: Netherlands, Lithuania, Baltics, Germany, Estonia, Sweden and Finland
2000	Merger of Falck and Group 4 into Group 4 Falck
2002	Acquisition of Wackenhut, USA

small and medium sized companies in Europe, South Africa and Canada. It also acquired 50% of Israel's largest security company. In parallel (2001), as part of its effort to become a more focused company, Group 4 Falck disposed of its contract cleaning business in Belgium and sold it to ISS. With a solid number two position and being the leading player in the ROW (Rest of the World), the company still needed to fill its market gap in the US market if it wanted to become a true global player. The opportunity arose when in March 2002 Group 4 Falck announced an agreed bid to take over the number two security company in the United States, Wackenhut (7% US market share, compared with Securitas' 20% market share).

The key events in Group 4 Falck's history are given in Table 2.2.

The Compass Group journey to leadership

Humble beginnings and an ordinary life (1941–1987)

Compass Group was founded in 1941 as Factory Canteens Ltd to feed munitions workers who, by legislation, were promised one hot meal a day. The food at work idea started during the Second World War, and marked the birth of the food services industry in the United Kingdom. In its first two decades, the now-called Compass Group grew along with the industry: steady and comparatively uneventful, essentially an entrepreneurial chronicle of private owners starting small firms and developing them gradually. A couple of consolidations in the 1960s and 1970s shaped the various companies that later become the Compass Group: in the 1960s, Grand Metropolitan, or 'Grand Met', a large spirits and hotel conglomerate, acquired the businesses that were the origins of Compass Group. In 1983, Grand Met merged and renamed the business Grand Metropolitan Catering Services. One year later, the firm was re-launched as Compass Group Services which included Compass Catering, Compass Security and Compass Cleaning. Gerry Robinson became the CEO and Francis Mackay became the CFO, and so began the most eventful decades in Compass Group's history.

The turning point (1987)

The turning point came in 1987 when Grand Metropolitan (now Diageo) disposed of its services division, Compass Group, through an MBO (management buy-out) priced at £163 million, which was then the largest MBO in UK annals. Since they co-invested in the MBO, the management team was among the new owners of Compass Group. At the time, Compass Group's yearly turnover was about £180 million, it employed about 20 000 people and, except for one contract in Alaska, it was strictly a UK company. In world ranking, it lagged far behind companies like ARA (now Aramark), Marriott's Catering Division, Eurest and Sodexho.

Pick your game (1987–1995)

Compass Group was a mish-mash: a catering business, a fairly large UK hospital business, a heating and ventilating engineering business and a building services company (security, maintenance, etc.). The management of the new company used the first years after the MBO to demonstrate its credentials as a company that could deliver against challenging financial targets. When Gerry Robinson left the group in 1991, Francis Mackay was appointed CEO. At this time he reviewed the company's strategy and embarked upon the plan of building a focused food service group on the international stage – no small ambition for a UK based company, since not many culinary experts admired English cuisine. Compass Group was a relatively large UK player, but it had no international experience in a market where the major players were Ara and Marriott from the United States, and Sodexho, Eurest, Gardner Merchant, SAS Service Partner and other European food service companies. Another handicap for Compass was its balance sheet which showed large borrowings as a result of the MBO.

Nevertheless, Compass Group, bolstered with confidence, set out to achieve its ambitious goals. It disposed of all its non food service operations, dumping the building service activities without a flinch. Shedding the hospital business, which consisted of private hospitals and nursing homes in the United Kingdom, was considerably more painful for Mackay because he had previously held Group responsibility for the hospital business.

In 1991, Gerry Robinson became the CEO of the much larger hotel and media group Granada Plc, and Mackay ascended to Chief Executive of Compass Group – as time would soon reveal, a prescient choice. Mackay, who grew up in Manor Park, North London, attributes his fabled gregariousness to growing up in a house tumbling with four boys. He picked up his financial training at a firm of accountants. After stretches in contract catering, a financial directorship of a travel business, Mackay was head-hunted into the contract catering division of Grand Metropolitan. The hail-fellow well-met, almost clubby ex-private pilot ('I got too big for the cockpits') has a mischievous sense of humour and loves people. He has what he himself calls a 'logical attitude to things, not particularly tough or hard nosed'.[1] Nevertheless, James Davis, a member of a law firm that has frequently represented Mackay, calls the Compass Group CEO 'an outstanding strategist...prepared to make brave, long-term decisions'. At Compass Group it didn't take long for Mackay to earn the reputation of level-headedness in the face of criticism.

Internationalization (early 1990s)

In the early 1990s Compass Group sent loud signals that it was going to expand to Europe. In 1992 the company was re-launched under a new identity and started a programme of expansion through organic growth and acquisitions with a clear strategy focusing on food service, segmentation, food service branding and international growth. Following the company's 'Right Direction' strategy, a wholly client-driven strategy that engendered sector-focused subsidiaries and innovative use of foodservice handling, Mackay then master-minded a number of big acquisitions in Scandinavia, America and then Europe and the rest of the world. At the same time, Mackay followed a programme of expansion through organic growth. The group already boasted a £345 million turnover, with 98.5% of operations in the United Kingdom. Although Compass Group had set out, theoretically at least, to go international with a cautionary start in Europe, unexpected events made the theory largely irrelevant. The internationalization of Compass Group, as it panned out, was anything but wary.

Industry shaping acquisitions (1992–present)

The reason that Compass Group largely skipped the phase of cautious internationalization was the opportunity to buy the non-airline catering

---

[1] Peston, Robert, 'Kingfisher is big DIY job for Mackay', *The Sunday Times*, 24 March 2002.

business of Copenhagen-based SAS Service Partner from SAS (Scandinavian Airlines System) in 1993. Suddenly the SAS Service Partner non-airline business, with operations in nine countries, was on the block, and Compass Group grabbed it. As institutional investors had been expecting Compass Group to focus on the larger countries in Europe, the SAS Service Partner acquisition surprised them all. But Service Partner was, in many ways, a very important acquisition for Compass Group since Service Partners' Scandinavian culture and its management team later made a lasting impact on the culture and style of the whole Compass Group.

Purchasing a non-core business from SAS was just the first of such acquisitions. During the next four years, the company went into accelerated growth mode in a big way. Investing £2.3 billion, the caterer scooped up 94 companies. The most publicized deals were: the US Canteen Corporation (1994) and Eurest from the French hotel group Accor (1995).

During the period between 1997 and 1998 shareholders expressed concern that the many acquisitions were diluting ROCE (Return on Capital Employed). So Mackay stopped acquiring for a while and let organic growth come through. In 1998 Compass Group landed a global contract with Philips Electronics, initially serving 110 000 Philips employees at 118 sites in Belgium, France, Germany, the Netherlands, Spain, the United Kingdom and the United States, with the opportunity to feed all 270 000 Philips employees the world over. In the same year, the North American division signed a deal with Microsoft for a countrywide contract encompassing 23 000 at 26 sites. In 10 years, with Mackay steering, the company has made over 100 acquisitions.

Francis Mackay may look like the quintessential nice guy, soft around the edges – his briefcase and the shapeless dog-eared satchel an Oxford Medieval scholar might lug around are statements of fashion modesty – but May 2000 proved him to be a man in a full metal jacket. Gerry Robinson, Mackay's old partner and friend, wanted to sell his catering and hotel businesses to Compass Group, but the deal would have hit Granada with a £1.5 billion tax bill. So Mackay and Robinson merged the two companies, then spun Compass Group off, along with the

Table 2.3 Key events in Compass Group history

1941	Group founded as Factory Canteens Limited
1968	Bateman and Midland Catering acquired by Grand Metropolitan and eventually merged as Grand Metropolitan Catering Services
1970	Eurest founded by Nestle´ and Wagon Lits
1984	Grandmet Catering re-launched as Compass Group Services
1987	Compass Group the then-largest UK management buy-out
1988	Compass Group PLC listed on the London Stock Exchange
1992	Compass Group launches 'The Right Direction'. Expansion through organic growth and acquisition. Acquires Letheby & Christopher and Travellers Fare
1993	Acquires Select Service Partner (then SAS Service Partner) from SAS Airlines
1994	Acquires Canteen Corporation
1995	Acquires Eurest International from Accor, disposes hospitals division
1997	Acquires SHRM, Daka
1998	First global foodservice contract with Philips to feed 270 000 staff. Joins FTSE 100 index. Acquires Restaurant Associates
1999	Michael Bailey appointed Group Chief Executive and Francis Mackay becomes Executive Chairman
2000	Acquires My Lunch and Riall of Italy. Partnership with Levy Restaurants. Merger with Granada Group creating Granada–Compass Group. Announces auction process for disposal of Forte Hotels
2001	De-merger of Granada–Compass Group. Compass Group re-listed on the London Stock Exchange. Acquired Morrison and Selecta
2002	Acquired Seiyo and Bon Appe´tit

Granada catering and hotel arms. Shareholders hated the deal. They argued that, by taking on a huge hotel portfolio that fitted awkwardly with its existing catering business, Compass Group was jeopardizing ten years of superlative growth.

With the Granada deal, Mackay brought down a rain of criticism on himself (it wasn't the first time). Headlines in the United Kingdom pilloried him, shareholders practically stoned him with acrimony, analysts savaged him and left him for the management mortuary. Marrying Granada was the epitome of foolishness, a sign that the level-headed pilot had made a mistake equivalent to landing without instruments at the wrong airport. Mackay pulled off the complex and controversial deal, silencing even the loudest of his critics, saved costs for Compass Group of £70 million per annum by year three, and raised a £3 billion war chest, giving the company enough ready cash for further acquisitions. Since then, Mackay has managed a series of international acquisitions and a number of divestitures. The company has gained a long list of new contracts, and has a catering contract retention rate in excess of 95%.

The key events in Compass Group's history are given in Table 2.3.

Sodexho's Journey to Leadership

Humble beginnings and an ordinary life (1966–1969)

In 1966, Pierre Bellon took over his father's maritime catering (ship chandlery) business in the old Mediterranean port of Marseille. From its decidedly *humble* origins with Bellon, the one van driver, shuttling up and down cobbled streets of Marseille, Sodexho widened its focus to include staff restaurants, schools and hospitals. Bellon worked for organic growth:

> *My first objective was, at the beginning, to enter a substantial market, with potential.*
>
> Pierre Bellon, Chairman, Sodexho Alliance

Bellon surrounded himself with high-quality staff, often graduates from his own Alma Mater, the Ecole des Hautes Etudes Commerciales (HEC) and gave them his full trust and total confidence. Nevertheless, quality problems dogged the company:

> *After a few months, I noticed that I was losing customers because the steak was overcooked and the chips too soft by the time I delivered them.*
>
> Pierre Bellon, Chairman, Sodexho Alliance

The lesson here was: 'to be more efficient, I had to be closer to the customer'. This conclusion led to Bellon's first corporate contract: all the catering for Baudouin, a now-defunct Marseille maker of boat engines. In 1968, operations commenced around Paris.

The turning point (1969)

Compared with all the other companies that have some significant size before they really pick their game, the turning point for Sodexho came almost 'immediately'. At the beginning of 1970, when the company was only four years old, still small (not even regional), Bellon received an unexpected call from an American who, without further ado, said, 'Mr Bellon, I would like to see you in Paris'.

'Who are you?' asked Bellon.

'Bill Fishman, President of Ara Services [now Aramark], number one in the world in catering services. I'm coming in my personal airplane, and I'd like to meet you.'

Bellon accepted, but 'what a surprise'. First of all, he could not imagine how Fishman had found him, since Sodexho was 'totally unknown'. Second, Bellon believed that catering, his 'métier', had been invented by the French!

In Paris, Fishman told Bellon he wanted to buy Sodexho, but Bellon put him off by suggesting that the two needed to get to know each other better. So Fishman invited Bellon to the United States (Philadelphia, Pennsylvania). Fishman opened Ara Services to Bellon, showing him Ara Services inside and out, and it was all 'very seductive'. During his 15-day visit, Bellon discovered a company that was 250 times bigger than Sodexho – for Bellon, an epiphany that had 'three major consequences'. First, he returned to France with a suitcase full of check-lists of procedures, policies and photos. Second, after seeing a successful company so much larger than his, Bellon was 'absolutely convinced' that Sodexho had 'considerable growth potential'. And third, seeing that the Americans already had a powerful 'landing force' for catering in Europe (Italy, Provence and Normandy), Bellon concluded that, unless he took action, the Americans would crush Sodexho. From this insight grew the simple

Sodexho strategy: plant the Sodexho flag as fast as possible in countries where US companies hadn't yet set foot – Belgium, Italy, the Middle East, Africa, Brazil. Meeting with Fishman had multiplied Bellon's ambition tenfold. Many years later, Bellon told Fishman, 'It was only because of you that we experienced our phenomenal growth.'

Pick your game (1966–1969)

Bellon has had the benefit of being the founder and owner all the way through the life of Sodexho. He has also had the benefit of defining his vision – being in food services – from day one. Contrary to the other three companies, he picked his game and played it from the day he founded the company. Over the years, as Bellon learned more and more about the market, however, the scope of the vision has evolved and expanded.

Internationalization (1969–1988)

During its first two decades of operation, Sodexho's overall growth strategy was organic growth (it still is). In 1971, International expansion began with a contract in Belgium for food service to a hospital. Soon after, the company started developing the remote-site management business, first in Africa and then in the Middle East, taking a decidedly opportunistic track. During this time, Sodexho's voucher business – providing vouchers for employee fringe and other social benefits – made its first sortie into Belgium and Germany. Bellon raced to Spain, Italy, Saudi Arabia and Brazil. He and his staff devised menus suitable for each geographic area. He hired local managers and encouraged them to act like entrepreneurs. He took initiative after initiative to keep customers happy. In each country, Sodexho had a single, clear vision: the company would not stop short of reaching number one or number two.

In 1983 Sodexho's IPO appeared on the Paris Stock Exchange. For the first few years, from 1985 to 1993, the group kept its anchors in France. Although it started up new activities in the Americas, Japan, South Africa and Russia, and reinforced its relatively small presence in Eastern Europe, it was still primarily oriented towards the French domestic market. By 1988, the company had grown to be number four worldwide.

Industry shaping acquisitions (1988–present)

At the time, Gardner Merchant, then the number one UK food services group, was doing 40 times Sodexho's business in the British Isles. Fearing that another company might snatch Gardner, Sodexho made a bold move: it acquired Gardner Merchant from the hotel group Trusthouse Forte, along with Partena, Sweden's premier contract management services provider, and became the world market leader in food services.

Sodexho shifted gear and moved from cautious internationalization to accelerated growth under Pierre Bellon's benevolent, but decisive, strong-willed leadership. Torben Sand, financial analyst at Svenska Handelsbanken in Copenhagen, describes the fatherly, resolute businessman Bellon as giving the company 'a very family and person-oriented profile'. Bellon's Sodexho essentially started from scratch in many countries. Sometimes this entailed acquiring companies in countries where it had started from nothing. An example is Brazil, where, after starting from nothing, Bellon engineered the acquisition of Wells, a 5000 employee catering business, from ISS. Bellon had his own strategy, always with his eyes on Compass Group, making forays into markets where no one else dared go. Bellon remembers: 'We started from scratch in France; we started from scratch in Belgium; we started from scratch in Italy. In a lot of countries, we started from scratch. [Solving all] our very big, very difficult problems gave us real competency and experience.'

One of Bellon's greatest strengths – according to Bernard Carton, his retired Vice President of Finance – is his ability to find the right people. Bellon himself says that his strength is to find and develop entrepreneurs. This skill has probably been *the* key to his success in opening up new markets.

Acceleration continued on the international stage. In 1996, the group's service voucher business took root in Brazil by acquiring Cardápio, the third largest service voucher supplier in Brazil. In 1997 the expanding group changed its name to the Sodexho Alliance. True to its new name, Sodexho Alliance joined forces with America's leading remote service provider, Universal Ogden Services. Patrice Douce, retired chief operating officer, Sodexho Alliance, explains: 'When you are French or British, and even more so if you are a Dane, your country is small compared with the United States. So if you want to grow, you have to grow outside your own boundaries. We [Sodexho] did some research, looked at the US market, which was the biggest, and saw that if we wanted to be a world player, we had to be in the US market.' True to this view, Sodexho bought a 48% stake in Sodexho Marriott Services (SMS), which was itself created by merging Marriott's contract catering business with that of Sodexho in North America. The new company was the market leader in North America for food and management services. Sodexho acquired a piece of Luncheon Tickets, the second biggest of the service vouchers in Argentina. Sodexho then quickly became number one in Chile by taking over the food and management services of Corpora. And Sodexho Alliance shares were accepted into the CAC40 index of the Paris Stock Exchange. The growth strategy in each of these countries was similar: segment and sub-segment the market to find new growth targets, and broaden the portfolio of offerings, from food services to multiservices containing anything from cleaning to medical services.

In 1998, Sodexho joined *Fortune*'s list of the world's 278 most admired companies (26 October 1998). A survey conducted by the Hay Group asked 5000 senior executives and financial analysts to rate companies on nine criteria: financial performance, overall management quality, product or service quality, innovativeness, value as a long-term investment, community responsibility, wise use of corporate assets, and effectiveness of doing business globally. Soon after, Sodexho Group launched the Sodexho Research Institute on the Quality of Life, an international initiative to identify consumer expectations for children, adolescents, adults and seniors. In Rome, Sodexho managed the world's largest-ever food service operation for the World Youth Day XV, serving three million pilgrims. The group also provided food services at the Olympic Games in Sydney, serving two million meals in Stadium Australia and supplying 90 000 meals at the sponsor's village.

Table 2.4 Key events in Sodexho history

1966	Pierre Bellon launches Sodexho
1977	International expansion starts in Belgium
1983	IPO on the Paris Stock Exchange
1983–1995	Sodexho starts activities in the Americas, Japan, South Africa and Russia, and reinforces its presence in Eastern Europe
1995	Sodexho acquires Gardner Merchant and Partena, becomes world leader in food service
1996	Sodexho acquires Cardápio, Brazil (service vouchers)
1997	Name change to Sodexho Alliance. Joins forces with Universal Ogden Services (USA)
1997	Acquires 48% stake in Sodexho Marriott Services (SMS), itself an amalgam of Marriott's contract catering services with Sodexho's in North America
1997	Sodexho acquires part of Luncheon Tickets, second largest service voucher company in Argentina and then Corpora, Chile's number one food and management services company
1997	Sodexho shares accepted on the CAC40 index of the Paris Stock Exchange
2000	Pierre Bellon steps down as CEO to become Chairman of the board
2001	Sodexho acquires 60% of Sogeres (France) from the Albert Abela Corporation and the remaining 40% of Sogeres from BNP PARIBAS Capital and all of Wood Dining Services (USA)
2001	Sodexho acquires Abela Holding France
2001	Sodexho acquires the remaining 52% of Sodexho Marriott Services

In spring 2001 Sodexho signed a contract with KPMG, the accounting firm, to provide cleaning and switchboard, as well as catering, to its Swedish subsidiary. In April 2001, Sodexho announced that it had signed an agreement with the Albert Albela Corporation to acquire 60% of Sogeres in France along with the entire share capital of Wood Dining Services in the United States. It also acquired the remaining 40% of Sogeres, managed by PAI management on behalf of PBN Paribas Capital. The combined purchase price was €526 million. Two months later, in June 2001, Sodexho announced the completion of its planned (since April 2001) acquisition of Abela Enterprises, the holding company of Wood Services in the United States. In June 2001 Sodexho also acquired the remaining 52% it did not already own in Sodexho Marriott Services.

The Sodexho story seen through the wide angle of almost four decades tells the tale of a typical entrepreneur, a fiercely independent but loyal spirit who cares above all else about people, demands loyalty, keeps bureaucracy to a slim minimum, and runs a tight ship. Bellon reduces much of Sodexho's progress to necessity and learning from mistakes. 'We say in French that we have "eaten our black bread". The sum of our success has been slightly bigger than the sum of our failures or mistakes. We learn more from our mistakes than from our success. But you know, the more I advance with the company, the more I have doubts.' He remains undaunted. 'Ask GE's Jack Welch,' he says without a trace of his Marseille accent, 'if his markets are mature. There are no mature markets, only bad managers.'[2] Two years after the turn of the century, Sodexho was the world's largest combined catering and facility services organization, present in 72 countries. The company serves seven million meals a day on five continents – as many as the entire population of Switzerland or Sweden – and, in its American river and harbour cruise business, runs boats in Norfolk and Richmond, Virginia, Washington, DC, Boston, New York, Philadelphia, Chicago and Seattle.

The key events in Sodexho history are given in Table 2.4.

Signposts 2002

Ten to 20 years ago the four companies were all fairly small and primarily local. They rarely hit the covers of business magazines. Their respective journeys have lifted them far beyond most other companies that were their 'equals' one to two decades ago, and they are today among the most admired services companies, all categories included. Take a moment to consider their achievements (see Figures 2.4 and 2.5).

---

[2]   Moukheiber, Zina, 'At your service', *Financial Times*, 1 November 1999.

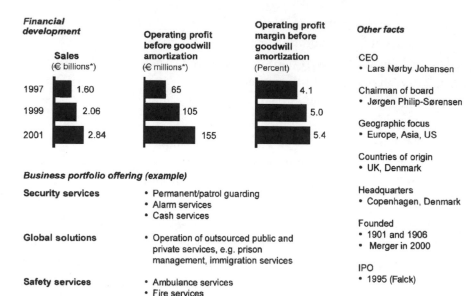

Figure 2.4 Group 4 Falck

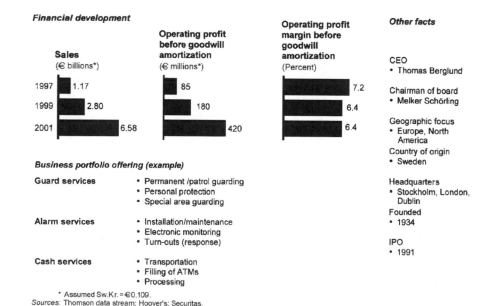

Figure 2.5 Securitas

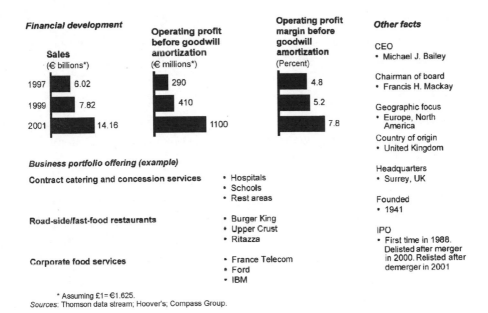

* Assuming £1= €1.625.
Sources: Thomson data stream; Hoover's; Compass Group.

Figure 2.6 Compass Group

Compass Group, Group 4 Falck, Securitas and Sodexho count among Europe's 20 largest companies, in numbers of employees – the same league as Siemens, Carrefour, Daimler–Chrysler and Unilever. Over the recent course of its journey, Securitas has become number one in Europe, the United States, and in the world. From 1997 to 2001, it has upped its sales from €1.17 billion to an expected €6.58 billion, and has millions of customers. Between 1997 and 2001, Group 4 Falck increased its sales from €1.60 billion to 2001 €2.84 billion. In early 2002, Group 4 Falck entered the US$14 billion US security market by acquiring Wackenhut, the second largest security provider in the United States and South America. As of 2002, Group 4 Falck had 215 000 employees in more than 80 countries. The company now focuses on security services, safety services and correction services. Compass Group is the world's largest food service and vending organization; in revenues, it is the largest food services provider in the world. In revenue, it is also the largest managed food services provider in the world. During the same 1997 to 2001 period, sales soared from €6.02 billion to a 2001 €14.16

billion. The company employs 360 000 people who work in more than 90 countries delivering contract catering and concession services, fast and road-side foods in chains like Burger King, Upper Crust and Ritazza, and corporate food services to the likes of France Telecom, Ford and IBM (see Figure 2.6).

In 2002, Sodexho Alliance is the world's largest combined catering and facility services organization (in revenue) with operations in 72 countries. Its client list includes corporations, colleges, hospitals and public institutions spanning the globe. In the half decade that closed out the 1990s, sales more than doubled, from €4.50 billion in 1997 to €11.94 billion in 2001. Food service contributes 90% of revenue with the remaining 10% arising from managed services facilities (ground maintenance, laundry), remote site management (offshore rigs), service vouchers and cards (in Europe and Latin America) and river and harbour cruises (a fleet of 40 boats in cities such as London and Paris) (see Figure 2.7).

SIGNPOST 2002

Financial development

Other facts

Sales (€ billions)	EBITDA (€ millions)	EBITDA margin (Percent)
1996/97 4.50	270	6.0
1998/99 9.03	580	6.4
2000/01 11.94	700	5.9

CEO
• Albert George

Chairman of board
• Pierre Bellon

Geographic focus
• Europe and North America

Country of origin
• France

Headquarters
• Montigny Le Bretonneux, France

Founded
• 1966

IPO
• 1983

Business portfolio offering (example)

Contract catering and concession services
• Hospitals
• Companies
• Schools

Sodexho Pass
• Vouchers
• Cards

Facility management
• Cleaning
• Reception
• Technical maintenance

Sources: Thomson data stream; Hoover's; Sodexho Alliance.

Figure 2.7 Sodexho Alliance

Four companies: Four winning traits

It is all about people . . . and it is therefore both simple and complex.
                                                        Waldemar Schmidt

Compass Group and Francis Mackay; Group 4 Falck and Lars Nørby Johansen and J. Philip-Sørensen; Securitas and Thomas Berglund; Sodexho Alliance and Pierre Bellon: each pair represents a steady, patient, unrelenting ascent to industry leadership. But by what means did Compass Group, Group 4 Falck, Securitas and Sodexho become numbers one and two? In the service industry, no magic wand, no special programme, no 'silver bullet', no radical or revolutionary management theory ensures successful, long-term growth. Success relies on: sustained rises in profit and stock price; employee loyalty and satisfaction; customer satisfaction and retention; the creation of superior shareholder value; industry leadership. So, in the words of Group 4 Falck's chairman J. Philip-Sørensen, success in service 'is about people, forget everything else'. But people need to be managed and guided; they need to know what to do, how to do it, and how to do it well time after time. And that brings us back to the central question: How have these four unheralded firms done so well? A close look at the histories of the companies reveals that although the book and verse of the four companies differs, there are similarities in their basic fibres.

The uniqueness of our high-performing service companies is consistency and superior execution along four simple dimensions, which we will describe in more detail in the coming chapters:

1. Pick Your Game and Play It
2. Leadership at the Heart
3. Passion for People
4. Keep It Simple

These four dimensions, in themselves, are not unique. Most service companies focus on people. But few really put enough management capacity (not only money but also time and attention) into the development of the employees in their organization and in their industries. Few stick to the task as single-mindedly as our four. They are doing nothing startlingly new – unless you consider doing the basics right over decades being something new. Just the basics, you might say. No, the uniqueness comes from the consistency, almost single-mindedness, with which the companies followed these four beacons, over the long haul. In the following four chapters we will take a closer look at each of these dimensions.

3

Pick your game and play it

Why do we talk so much about focus? If you run a manufacturing company, you build your production line and once you place the various kinds of machinery in the line, they stay there. People don't stay where you put them. They move around all the time so it takes a much stronger focus to make them continue to perform than it takes to make the production line continue to perform because it just does the same thing every day. You just push the On button and it runs. But people move around, they have to provide a different service every day, and that's why focus is even more important in services than it is in manufacturing.

Thomas Berglund, CEO, Securitas

Astronomers will tell you that the Earth wobbles as it spins. Irregularities in the Earth's rotation – small oscillations superimposed on larger wobbles atop even larger wobbles – cause the location of the 'true' North Pole to wander across the arctic landscape. Many service companies suffer from oscillations. They start with a clear focus on their own true north, but eventually they wobble and waggle and lose focus, gradually meandering across the service industry landscape. Not so Compass Group, Group 4 Falck, Securitas and Sodexho. What's the difference? The answer is: focus.

Our four companies pick their game and play it. Consider Securitas. It was originally on its way to becoming a multiservices company in Sweden. It 'wobbled' into manufacturing locks and gates, and all sorts of security gadgets, and digressed into cleaning. But it later disposed of its non-security businesses, such as lock manufacturing and cleaning. Securitas today hones in solely on security services (including cash in transit, alarm systems and Securitas Direct).

Group 4 Falck targets security services *and* safety services. Compass Group focuses on food service and vending to groups and individuals, including roadside restaurants and concessions, but excluding, for example, cleaning or anything to do with vouchers. Sodexho concentrates on food services *and* extended services for existing clients (they call this combination 'multiservice') which include additional services that existing food service clients might require, for example cleaning. Sodexho is not in the concession business.

Compass Group, Group 4 Falck, Securitas and Sodexho follow a simple formula for business success: *decide what you want to do – and what you don't want to do – then do it well*. To varying extents, the companies have narrowed their focuses. Despite the many temptations to add so-called 'related' services, and therefore complicate their businesses unnecessarily, all have simplified their complex business into a clear, organizing idea, made sure employees understand it, and have then given them the wherewithal to turn the idea or vision into a working strategy. The width of their angle of focus varies considerably: from Sodexho's very broad mission to 'improve the quality of life for people' down to the narrower focus of Securitas, which wants to 'protect homes, work places and the community'.

The two company founders in *Winning at Service*, Bellon and Sørensen, have always had clear visions for Sodexho and Group 4 Falck (or its progenitors), but the hired CEOs, Mackay, Nørby Johansen and Berglund, did not necessarily *start* with a clear vision or winning strategy. Thomas Berglund and Francis Mackay even said they started with no visions, or even a different one from today's, but within six to twelve months they had formulated a vision that ran contrary to the industry vision of the time. For security firms, the trend was to expand the portfolio, offer many different kinds of services, but Securitas chose to focus on security services only. For food service, the trend was multiservice – Sodexho followed this track to rapidly grow sales. Mackay chose to focus on food services only and to increase the top line first. The founders Sørensen and Bellon didn't narrow their services palette as much as Berglund, Nørby Johansen and Mackay. But the five leaders have all provided the people in their respective companies with clarity at both the macro level (what business do we want to be in?) and at the micro level (who are our customers and to what extent can we best serve their needs).

Each of the four companies has wrought a *replicable business model* – one more defined and communicated than the others – that has worked in small, local markets. They have all improved and refined these business models on a local scale, and then, riding and creating a wave of outsourcing at the same time, applied them in new locations or in acquired companies. Replicable business models comprise simple but effective processes, concepts and tools that support the most essential elements in the service delivery process and allow for local adaptation. Whatever each company calls these tools and processes, they give managers in the widely dispersed networks concepts that they can use to make their own decisions within the parameters of cost efficiency and high-quality service.

To keep an organization of more than 200 000 or even 300 000 staff on course, top management has to make sure that every manager in the organization has a clear idea of how his or her unit in the company is performing. The companies have identified some key levers that every manager applies in the form of clear and simple performance measures. Imagine that our companies' managers are left pretty much on their own at thousands of service sites in places as far apart as Minneapolis and Moscow. These managers need to know how they are doing and how their performance slots into the big picture of the company. *Simple, transparent performance measures* support the clarity. But this clarity does not benefit the site managers only; it is just as important for the senior management team. The companies keep these measures simple and consistent all over the world so that when the compounded results land on senior managers' desks, they can easily sift through all the information to spot those all-important warning signs that the company, or parts of it, might be veering off course.

Decide what you want to do

Compass Group: Branded food service to groups and individuals

Francis Mackay and his team have taken a long-term stance of not diversifying managed services beyond on-site services. Compass Group took the decision long ago to derive all its revenues from food services and vending activities unless facilities management services are required by the sector (such as in health care and remote sites). According to Michael Bailey, the company has never strayed from its core:

> We are a food service contract business. We do not see ourselves running a main street restaurant company . . . we do not see ourselves going that far away from the core guts of the business. We do not see ourselves as a one-size-fits-all answer.
>
> Michael J. Bailey, CEO, Compass Group

Compass Group's food service focus (at first, mainly for corporate and public service clients only) includes the concession business and roadside restaurants in which it serves individuals in captive and semi-captive environments. Mackay believes that people who on Saturday night go to Pizza Hut will also want to go to Pizza Hut during the week – at work in their company's restaurant, in the hospital where they visit a family member or where they are a patient, or at the airport. To be able to develop brand equity for retail brand concepts, Compass Group moved into the semi-captive concession market. Strategically, this meant facing the clients with brands they would identify over time as professional, in which they had confidence, and for which they would pay a higher price. Mackay notes that Compass Group has chosen a different route from its main competitors:

> We have gone a slightly different route. What we have is the mainstream contract service route – corporate, healthcare, and education – and we have added the concession and the retail brand concepts. Our competition has gone for the facilities management process, which is on the other side. They have been driven by the characteristics of the contracts; we have been driven by the requirement to develop the brand equities.
>
> Francis Mackay, Chairman, Compass Group

According to Mackay, Healthcare and remote site services are the only sectors that allow for multiservice:

> Only healthcare and remote sites are slightly different. Food services is a more value-added product than cleaning or portering, and the danger of combining them is that you tend to move to the lowest common denominator. So we retain the catering focus while at the same time recognizing that in one sector it is changing

slightly, then we can do that as an add-on, but not integrate it into the company. Management training and structures are different for different products, so if you integrate them, you lose the way.

Francis Mackay, Chairman, Compass Group

An industry marketing expert commented that Compass Group has benefited from the fact that it has been very focused on a few well-defined activities. 'There are lots of temptations to go into cleaning and security.' The marketer pointed out that, although some parts of the business have broadened, essentially forcing Compass Group to do deals with cleaning and security companies to get contracts in the healthcare segment, by and large it is known that Compass Group keeps its focus on food service and vending. 'That's where it all starts.'

Sodexho: Inventing and providing services to improve clients' quality of life

Patrice Douce, a Sodexho veteran, says the secret to Sodexho's growth is 'a clear vision of where we want to go and a clear strategy of how to get there'. Over the years, people have bombarded the management with suggestions: why don't you go upstream, buy a factory, or maybe a logistics company to transport the food you deliver?' 'No,' said Sodexho, 'we have a clear vision and a consistent strategy. And the will to do it.'

Compared with the focus of the other three companies, on the other hand, Sodexho's definition of its game seems almost all-encompassing:

Invent and provide, all over the world, every kind of service that can bring to individuals, living in society together, a more pleasant existence at any moment in their lives.

Pierre Bellon, Chairman, Sodexho Alliance

Whereas Sodexho refuses offers to go upstream or downstream, it does not say no to clients' requests for extended services:

In order to keep our clients, we deliver other services: first in food services we have a lot of services, including, for example, the take-out for the employees. But we also have expanded into what we call the 'multi-service' . . . Another example is that we

*can manage, in the big headquarters, the fitness clubs or we can do the laundry for
the people – exactly as in a hotel, where you have a laundry service . . . we can do
that. That is what we call 'people services'.*

Sodexho Yearly Report

Sodexho claims that with these extended services it creates value in three ways.

1. The company helps clients use their sites more efficiently and productively. 'In the UK we rent our reception facilities at Royal Ascot for conventions, conferences, and gala evenings.'
2. The company also works to make the client's employees more efficient and productive. 'We have created a shop, for example, that makes working life and personal life more comfortable by offering such services as dry cleaning, car maintenance, domestic help and take-away food. We run errands to government agencies that are only open during employee working hours.'
3. Sodexho does whatever it can to enhance the client's reputation and image. 'At Loyola University, USA, we offered an ambitious programme of renovating buildings, improving food services, and creating pleasant areas where students could gather. Enrolment increased 30%.'

In food and management services, Sodexho's original offer engendered pretty much run-of-the-mill traditional catering for business and industry, healthcare, education and retirement homes; in 2002 the company offered a much wider palette, with new catering segments like prestige events, multiservice on remote sites, and detention and correction services.

Take, for example, a client in the company's business and industry segment: a construction firm with 125 000 employees worldwide and with some 350 in the head office. Across the world, Sodexho provided them with an array of eating options, from a buffet set up on a remote construction site to a luxurious restaurant for executives and their clients. These services come as part of an agreed contract. At some stage, the clients (this is important – Sodexho extends its services only for existing clients) may want Sodexho to take care of its coffee services, or vending machines or special conference banquets, as well. Sodexho calls all these add-ons 'extra services', and bills them separately from the main food service contract.

Some clients want to outsource even more activities and ask Sodexho to take care of their laundry needs, ground maintenance and even some administrative functions such as a mailroom. Another good example of this approach was Ripon College, a client in Wisconsin, USA. The small liberal arts college selected Sodexho to provide a comprehensive package of food, maintenance and facilities management services. The benefits, according to Dr Paul Ranslow, Ripon's President, included much better service quality.

Teams that traditionally tend to compete with each other have created their own special synergy. Since they work for the same company, food service employees and other service staff share the same commitment to contributing to overall quality of the college. Whether it's to provide logistic support, lend a piece of equipment, or share a team member, everyone works easily and effectively together, especially when organizing major events like graduation.

Dr Paul Ranslow, President of Ripon College, Wisconsin, USA

In a hospital, Sodexho can provide all the services that a hotel provides. Sodexho suggests that you can view a hospital as a 'medical services centre plus hotel facilities'. The company allows the doctors and medical staff to get on with healing, to concentrate on their technical and medical responsibilities, and leave Sodexho to do the rest. Universal Sodexho plays a similar role on remote sites such as oil platforms and remote construction sites where extended services are very much in demand – clients are delighted to have one provider. These are Sodexho's 'extended services', and the total package is 'multiservice'.

Sodexho people stress that this strategy is not about diversification: Sodexho will not provide mailroom or laundry service to a client who does not yet use its food services. What happens, we asked, when a potential customer that works with another food service provider wants Sodexho's extended services? 'Sodexho will not immediately jump on the opportunity, but it will make a total package proposal – including food services – to this potential customer.'

Where before Sodexho offered only meal tickets in its services and vouchers segments, it now proffers meal, gift, gasoline and medicine tickets.

Cruises and meals in the new river and harbour cruises segments now complement the more typically-related offers. When it comes to new people services, Sodexho has positioned itself in vending, room and conference services, cleaning and maintenance, and telephone, reception and call centre. Its business services encompass office space allocation management, moving services, mail collection and delivery, and shipping and handling. This list does not even touch on the company's relatively new building utilities maintenance and management services. In 1998, new services had a turnover of €534 million, or 7% of total turnover. For 2000–2001, Sodexho did €11.9 billion in business, of which 97% was in food and management services: 46% business and industry; 18% healthcare; 5% seniors; 23% education; and 5% remote sites.

Securitas: Security service its game, the industry its playground

When in 1984 Thomas Berglund was recruited as financial manager of one of the Securitas regions, he 'basically understood nothing about security, had no vision about what to do'. The security industry was plagued by low, uneven quality in the delivery of service offerings, a narrow range of service offerings, evidence of criminal records among some companies and employees – making it a pretty rough business, and many small players, only a few of which were international. Few people considered working for the security industry a profession. At that time Securitas badly needed more revenue and had to find a way to make the business profitable.

The company took what seemed to be the sensible course of action: focus on security service and security *service* only.

> *You could say that our strategy was taken 17 years ago when we decided to focus on security service, and the rest is just a consequence of that decision. Seventeen years ago, the wisdom of the age was that you should not focus, not specialize, you should broaden, go for multiservice. You should use your customer base to deliver different things from what you were doing, so companies should go for cleaning or catering or helping the elderly. Today that's called facility management but it adds up to doing everything for everyone. We felt it was challenging enough to become professional in just one area: security.*
>
> Thomas Berglund, CEO, Securitas

Figure 3.1

This decision became a pillar of Securitas' strategy and, later, one of the basic tenets of the company's business model (see Figure 3.1):

Focus on security was the most important decision. Remember: it's so easy to get excited, I mean there are a lot of beautiful ideas especially when you meet a lot of clever people. They can come up with an endless number of ideas. But maybe it's not up to us to do everything. When you focus on security you can use your energy to understand your different customer segments.

Thomas Berglund, CEO, Securitas

Securitas sold off other businesses and, for a few years, spent all its management attention on developing a superior business model in order to become a security industry leader in its existing markets:

When we decided to focus on security, we decided not to go for the whole world, at least not in one shot, but to focus in a few markets to become market leader in those markets. First we spent 10 years becoming the market leader in most European countries, and now we've started to be market leader in North America. It's important, especially in the service industry, for someone to take the lead and guide the industry on where to go, and how to do things and how to develop, also including teaching the customers what they should ask for, because a well-educated customer is a better customer.

Thomas Berglund, CEO, Securitas

Group 4 Falck: Security and safety

Before the merger with Falck, Group 4 was in the global security service business – like Securitas – but it also had its global solutions business; facility management contracts with public institutions, mostly in the United Kingdom.

Global Solutions (GSL), one of the three Group 4 Falck businesses, involves what the company calls Public Private Partnerships (PPP) contracts and Private Finance Initiative (PFI) projects. This market offers many benefits, particularly long-term contracts (10, 15, 20 years and more) and true partnership arrangements with clients. The idea is to 'create an environment in which clients can concentrate on their core activities'. With Global Solutions, Group 4 Falck tries to provide total solutions to its customers' requirements: IT problems downwards and cleaning problems upward. Set up in a number of business streams, GSL brings a new kind of people to the company, with higher skills than the company has had before: contractual people, life cycle engineers, healthcare experts and many others.

Prior to its merger with Group 4, Falck was Scandinavia oriented, focused on safety, and was trying to expand its game to security. Many Scandinavians considered Falck a part of the public sector, a public institution of some sort, part of the country's healthcare system. It was not. CEO Lars Nørby Johansen explained that if Falck wanted to develop into an international player and become less dependent of the public sector in Denmark, it had to grow a business alongside safety:

From an operational point of view and a conceptual point of view, the two businesses, safety and security, go very well with each other. Security has to do with preventing accidents from occurring, whatever kind – fire, burglary, whatever – whereas safety is making sure that help is at hand if something goes wrong – and as we all know, sadly, something does go wrong once in a while. To fulfil customers' needs for security it's not enough to focus on prevention only, you must also focus on safety. There is an operational reason, too. Look at the fit between safety and security. Security is pretty active at night; in safety our people are active in daytime. Combining the two businesses gives a lot of synergies, cross-synergies really. We can cross-utilize our resources much more effectively than if we had had just one service.

Lars Nørby Johansen, CEO, Group 4 Falck

When Group 4 and Falck merged, despite the usual tough negotiations before signing, it appeared relatively natural for the two companies to blend and become one truly global player with one definition of the game it would play: the game of both safety and security. The company follows that definition with an almost religious fervour:

Compared with other companies' management, this company is good at prioritizing, and we are persistent. When we have made a priority, taken a decision – even if we run into disappointment – we stick to the strategy. We do not zigzag. Consistency is the way things are managed and executed. It is not only a question of performing; it is based on fairness, fairness towards leaders and employees, and also towards those who actually pay your salary, the shareholders.

John Dueholm, former COO of Group 4 Falck and
as of 1 September 2002, Executive Vice President SAS,
Scandinavian Airline Systems

Follow a simple, replicable business model

Group 4 Falck

Group 4's business model was very much built on the entrepreneurial spirit of its owners:

I chose the route of going to countries where there wasn't much competition. It was harder in the beginning but you made a name much quicker in those countries. I had to go and convince people that we were a service organization, and any modern society needs a modern services organization. People like to hear about new businesses, particularly when you are a young man from a foreign country. At first they say 'What is this man doing here? Selling security services. We have the armed forces and the police. We don't need any private armies.' But in the end, they did see my point.

J. Philip-Sørensen, Chairman of the Board of Directors, Group 4 Falck

This entrepreneurial business model made Group 4 a worldwide security provider, present in many more countries than its competitors. Sørensen does concede that the 'business model' was not as deliberately chosen as it might seem:

I'd like to say that growing the business in Group 4 organically by going to new countries and starting up was a very clever philosophy, but that wouldn't be entirely true. The truth is more that I had to make the cash to develop, and it is cheaper to develop a company from scratch than walking up and making a major acquisition. When you make a major acquisition as a private company, you are bound to the banks – they own you at the end. And I come back to one of my grandfather's rules again: 'Never borrow more from your bank than you can pay back in five minutes without going to jail.' That was the reason I started building up from scratch in most countries.

J. Philip-Sørensen, Chairman of the Board of Directors, Group 4 Falck

Deliberate or not, by the year 2000, Sørensen's business was attractive enough for Falck to consent to a merger. Falck has followed the same mission ever since 1906: to provide safety to the general public; to prevent accidents; to provide assistance in situations of need; and to limit losses and save property. The merged company's business model is based on creating synergies from the merger by offering clients an all-inclusive package in safety and security:

We have three business areas: security, safety, and global solutions. For example, in Sweden we have a contract in a car factory where we do all the security, but we have a new contract to do the firefighting inside the factory, in case of fire. We are moving up the value chain: you have guards and you educate them as firemen. It is good for the client, good for our employees, and good for the company's business.

Nels Petersen, Group Communications Director, Group 4 Falck

Securitas

As we have seen in Chapter 2, The Journey to Leadership, Securitas expanded carefully by following the same business model everywhere:

We took it step by step, first Sweden, then Europe and finally, in 1999, the leap over the Atlantic. By then, all of the pieces were in place in our minds.

Thomas Berglund, CEO, Securitas

SECURITAS' STEP-BY-STEP APPROACH

Step 1: FOCUS – Get the organization and structure and people in order
Begin from the ground up by creating the right organization and structure and recruiting the right people into key positions. Clearly delegated responsibility, cost controls, and reliable financial follow-up are crucial before proceeding further.

Step 2: REFOCUS – Work on existing core business
Focus on existing operations. Analyse each workflow to raise quality and efficiency. Visits, interviews and working close to customers increases the understanding for security needs.

Step 3: BECOME MARKET LEADER IN CURRENT MARKETS – Refine and tune
Refine and specialize operations and develop them in every area. Specialization creates a focus on a single service or product designed for a specific customer segment. The more Securitas learns about the security needs of its various customers the better it will understand how to sell, produce and follow up its products and services. Here, quality and training work is also emphasized.

Step 4: INFLUENCE THE INDUSTRY IN THAT MARKET – Think about organic growth and acquisitions
Now the focus turns to organic growth through intensified sales efforts. At the same time, specialization and development work continues. This is also the right time for new acquisitions, when the process turns to step one again.

Figure 3.2 The Securitas toolbox

Since the mid-1980s, the Securitas business model has remained the same, but near the end of the 1990s the company captured its model in a tangible form, a visual and tactile aid, that Securitas managers use all the time: 'the Securitas toolbox' (Figure 3.2).

The Securitas toolbox is an actual wooden box with the Securitas three-red-dot logo on the top, heavy black hinges and a thick rope handle – the sort of hand-crafted container you'd stuff with life vests, C-rations and flares, and stow below the decks of a sailboat. And in that sense, perhaps it looks like what it is: a box full of the only things you'll need to survive, even prosper, not when the sailing gets tough, but when business gets tough. Inside are eight wooden pieces of various shapes and sizes: cubes, a miniature circus tent, two hands, the simple figure of a person, and a few flat pieces that look like learning toys from a primary school geometry lesson. These are the eight so-called 'tools'. Each represents a philosophy, a mission, a whole array of thoughts and guidelines to help Securitas' managers and employees better understand the drivers of the security business and the company's business model (see Figure 3.3).

> *Over the years we developed different elements, each of them on its own quite obvious, but we never thought about combining them [into a package] . . . we had it together as a kind of management theory and we used it for our internal training. The thinking behind these solid wooden figures was that people could actually put them on their desk, use them in talks with staff or plainly for their own inspiration.*
> *Thomas Berglund, CEO, Securitas*

The toolbox isn't merely a manager's practical treasure chest, it is a vehicle for improving communication. All 2000 branch managers have their own. Every new manager gets one. The company expects them to use the tools extensively to ensure consistent customer approach and service delivery. But how do managers actually use it?

Kris Van den Briel, Division Manager in Belgium, got the toolbox at the 2000 Senior Executives Meeting:

> *What is fascinating about the toolbox is to see how different parts of the business can create a complete picture of the business. Finance alone is not what it's all about . . . We are an organization that has always looked for concepts to make things clear to people, and for simple but logical tools to use when dealing with problems. . . . Take the Market Matrix for example. It is a valuable tool for analysing your own portfolio – what you're good at or where you have strong development.*
> Kris Van den Briel, Division Manager, Securitas

Tony Sabatino, Area Manager in Securitas USA, uses the toolbox all the time, in his role both as an educator and as a manager:

> *It helps me evaluate what I'm doing as I'm doing it. With the ten managers who report to me, I use it as educator and coach. They have had training from a textbook perspective, but now I can help them apply the tools in their daily work. The way the toolbox is set up makes it very easy for me to relate to branch managers and security supervisors (usually guards who have stayed with the company several years). For example, the step-by-step process has really simplified what most of us who went to business school understand. The value chain is the most difficult tool to explain to managers because it is difficult to manage clients differently from how they have been managed in the past*
> Tony Sabatino, Area Manager, Securitas

When we asked Chantal Austin, a Securitas Regional Manager for Normandy in France, if she used the toolbox, her reply was:

> *Of course! In every day of work. Also in meetings with our managers, especially the six fingers and the step-by-step model as we sometimes have difficulties in keeping things really simple. The guards know about the tools – though they do not use them on site – they are used in meetings at the branch office. For example, the one about running the industry. Our French CEO has taken the role of running the industry very seriously, and this has had a direct effect on the guards as he has managed to change the collective agreement by raising wages, and more recently to obtain extra pay for night work. This is not easy, as you have to not only convince*

1. Values: First of all, set the focus. Our focus is security, and our mission is to protect homes, workplaces and communities. This is the cornerstone and it is important that we all share the same values.

2. Market matrix: Then you have to understand the market. Who are the customers? The market matrix shows the size of the customers, the types of businesses they are in and the extent of their security needs. There is a difference between the security needs of a bank and an oil company, even if they are both big, and within the big oil company there are different needs for the oilrig, the head office and the gas station.

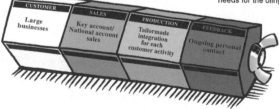

3. Value chain: Once you have understood what the customer needs, you have to set the standards for how to interact with each customer. For instance, a large customer will require a key account manager at the sales stage, customized integration for each activity and ongoing personal contact during the follow-up stage. And this is not the way you should interact with a private person who wants an alarm kit for the home.

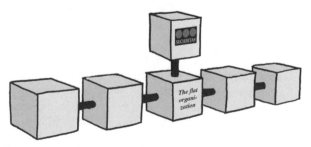

4. Flat organization: A centralized organization is not stable. Therefore the Securitas organization is a flat one and, with the right person in the right place, it is efficient and creates strong personal commitment.

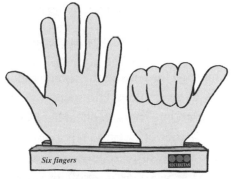

5. Six fingers: At this stage it is time to measure performance. The six fingers represent six factors that affect Securitas' result. Why fingers? When we wanted to establish key figures for that, we started to count on our fingers and we ended up with five. Later on, we added one more – the golden one – because of late payment issues in some countries.

6. Industry: Once you have your company in order it is time to consider the operating environment. Someone has to grow strong enough to run the industry, to take responsibility. It's about wage levels, training standards, regulations and a lot more. We believe that having a significant influence on the community, police and authorities helps us to develop a healthy industry, which in turn makes us grow.

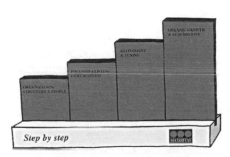

7. Step by step: All the items above can't be carried out at the same time. The seventh tool is a four-step staircase to growth and success. Step by step is a matter of doing things in the right order, at a pace that allows the company to grow. It starts with getting your organization and business in order, to grow organically and when you finally get to the point where you grow by acquisition, it starts all over again from step one.

8. People make the difference: Finally, it's you who make the difference. And here is how: Understanding comes with the mind, commitment with your heart. Keep it simple by following your gut feeling. And last but not least, be a good example by leading the way.

Figure 3.3 The Securitas business model. Source: Securitas Management Bulletin, Issue 2, May 2000

your customers, but your competitors, too. The battle for extra pay for night and weekend work has cost us three years.

Chantal Austin, Regional Manager, Securitas

Securitas has created a step-by-step method for putting the toolbox ideas into practice, and this is the essence of its real value. The success of the company's step-by-step tool underpins our finding that a replicable business model, no matter how it's defined, and whether or not it is represented by some tangible wooden figures, is vital for a widely dispersed service business. The 'step-by-step' approach illustrates how Securitas goes about growth and, more particularly, about integrating new acquisitions. First Securitas identifies its favourite sort of acquisition targets: 'tired market leaders' (in Berglund's terms), under-performers with turnaround potential. It acquires the object of its desire, buys low-priced stock with high-priced Securitas stock or cash and then, using the step-by-step approach, it creates a new foundation for growth and profitability.

Compass Group

According to a senior marketing expert, Compass Group is the world leader in its industry because of its very clear and simple and consistent (year after year) strategy that's easy to communicate and that everybody from the top down understands. Broken into four elements, Compass Group's consistent strategy looks like this:

1. Focus on food service and vending
2. Target sectors
3. Develop internationally/geographically
4. Use food service brands

Says the marketing director, 'I have worked in companies that have a great strategy and then next year they change it. This is not the case in Compass Group.' Let's have a closer look at Compass Group's vision on brands. Despite the traditional sap running through its core, Compass Group is in no way traditional in the way it approaches its brand name strategy. Instead of trying to build brand equity of the Compass Group name, it has created what it calls 'specialist companies' for each segment (business and industry, education, fine dining, health care, retail and leisure, sports and events, travel, vending), with each company operating relatively independently and with its own corporate structure. Part of Compass Group business model is to allow these separate companies to have their own business model.

Most of the acquired companies (such as, for example, Eurest) have kept their original name and, while picking up some sweeping characteristics of the Compass Group, have also maintained at least some semblance of their original culture. This means that although most staff who work for Eurest know that Eurest manages their food service operation, many of them may not even know that Eurest is owned by a company called Compass. A director at a local elementary school would probably have no clue that her school's food services are provided by the same company that provides food for the working mothers and fathers of many of the pupils. You won't find a common logo tying all these companies together. This – by the way – does not mean that Compass Group ignores latent economies of scale: the company's purchasing department has already created many economies of scale and you may well find an Upper Crust sandwich outlet (one of Compass Group's internal brands) next to a Taco Bell kiosk in both Eurest and a Scolarest account.

Sodexho

Other than its non-compromising attitude to quality and fair price levels, the Sodexho business model is relatively flexible: 'Listen to the clients first.' As Patrice Douce put it:

> You have clients who have their own philosophy, such as 'Our core business is such and such, and we want to outsource the rest. And we would be better off to have one supplier, because it's cheaper and easier.' Other customers or clients say 'We outsource certain things but not others because we consider that is part of our image.' Others say, 'Even though we are in favour of outsourcing, we want to spread our risk so we won't give too many things to one supplier.' So, I think we need to listen. We have no dogma.
>
> Patrice Douce, retired COO, Sodexho Alliance

Sodexho focuses on organic expansion. At the same time, the group has developed a taste for strategic international alliances and acquisitions, especially when it comes to potential partners who share its business mission. This policy is rooted in respect for the history, cultures, and personalities of the men and women who join the group. Says Hans Rijnierse:

> When they acquired us in 1995, they really did not change a lot. The only major change that happened almost immediately was the introduction of Sodexho's 'five step approach' in purchasing. This change was for the better, it helped us improve relations with suppliers and increased efficiency in purchasing. Otherwise we were performing well, so Sodexho let us use our 25-year-old success formula and only introduced some new reporting procedures. They know that country management will lose some of its commitment for the business if the head office decides for them.
>
> Recently management asked me to share my expertise with 25 European managers in a training programme. This type of best practice sharing gives me a feeling of mutual respect.
>
> Hans Rijnierse, Managing Director Sodexho The Netherlands
> and Deputy Chairman Sodexho South Africa.

Use simple, transparent performance measures

Securitas

Between the late 1980s and 2002, Securitas management continued to develop the business model, but they were always bothered by the complexity of the many performance measures in the company and they found it difficult to get managers to understand what was really indicating the business's progress. At some point – Berglund doesn't recall the precise ah-ha moment, or even if there was one – he and his managers got the idea that if they could visualize the company's key performance indicators, people would remember them better:

> We were sitting around a table on a dark November evening in 1987. Melker Schörling, Carl-Henric Svanberg, Hakan Winberg (CFO) and I were trying to understand the monthly reports – people came in with big boxes of computer papers

and told us 'this is your monthly report'. We couldn't figure out what was up and what was down. So we asked ourselves, 'What do we really want to know to understand our performance?' Talk went back and forth – 'this and this and this' – and suddenly we had five things that had a lot to do with the volume development of the portfolio, the stock of contracts. We called it 'Five fingers'.

Thomas Berglund, CEO, Securitas

But how were more than 2000 operations people who didn't have a degree in accounting to understand how the numbers come together? Securitas' senior management was convinced – this is a Securitas principle – that a clear understanding of the numbers is a prerequisite for decentralizing a company.

The more you complicate the business, the fewer will understand it, and the more power you will have to centralize. And the more you centralize, the less dynamics you will get out in the field where the people that produce are. So the very simplistic five fingers helped the 2000 branch managers run their businesses.

Thomas Berglund, CEO, Securitas

To the five performance measures that lead to the operating result (new sales, net change, invoicing, margin and cost) Securitas added a sixth measure – 'receivables' – an indicator of the cash flow at the country level.

Group 4 Falck, Sodexho and Compass Group: Balanced scorecard

Both Compass Group and Group 4 Falck use the balanced scorecard as their leading performance measurement tool. The details of the key indicators remain confidential, but Compass Group revealed some of the high-level measures. The Compass Group scorecard measures customer satisfaction (individuals), client satisfaction (companies), employee satisfaction, and financials, for example. Mackay says the company has a key performance indicator manual about what is important. The manual tells everybody, from the Board right on down the business to a restaurant site manager, what matters in Compass Group . . . We can actually measure exactly where the business is going: not just about margin, but also about the level of employee turnover, the level of employee satisfaction in Catalonia, customer satisfaction, financial results.

Mackay told us that implementing Compass Group's strategy was a 'challenge', but that managing quality wasn't so tough. There was just the risk of 'getting it wrong' as the company ballooned with acquisition after acquisition that loomed large.

With the balanced scorecard, Compass Group had a tool that 'operationalizes' everything that it measures:

> *Sure, sales growth is important; of course margin is important, but what else? . . . the balanced scorecard includes all the other factors. It is a tremendous boost to the business. It is the mechanism by which we manage the business now. It focuses the whole of the management team, from the Chairman right on down to the restaurant manager, on more than just financial results. It's a whole process of information coupled with a whole process that answers the question, 'How do we change it?'*
>
> Francis Mackay, Chairman, Compass Group

Sodexho also uses a tool that resembles a balanced scorecard. During its last decade of turbo-growth, Sodexho defined mandatory quality standards across the group. It instituted continuous tracking of quality improvement indicators – satisfaction surveys and restaurant tracking rates, for example. Working with research from independent organizations, internal audit teams and employees, the company continuously identifies areas for improvement. Sodexho applies and shares a few key value creation drivers that have 'long been at the heart of the management philosophy, values and strategies'. Because the company is decentralized, understanding and evaluating these business decision drivers lies at the heart of what the company likes to call its 'Sodexho entrepreneur' culture. Managers in the operating divisions use simple decision-support tools and simulation models 'to measure the alternative impacts of various strategies on key indicators'. Not only group management, but also country managers, segment heads, regional directors, and district and site managers track operational performance indicators, which are also part of both measuring past performance and long-term planning and decision-making. The indicators focus on:

- Client retention, market share gains, additional on-site services and sustainable sales growth.

- Innovation, employee retention, purchasing efficiency, and other sources of operating profitability.
- Taxation and capital being employed efficiently – notably in working capital management.
- Generation of free cash flow.

As of 2001, group management had created a Planning and Strategic control Department to enhance these success factors and share best practices, coordinate, transfer skills and monitor operational performance indicators.

Questions for service leaders

1. What type of game have you picked for your company? And what have you actively decided *not* to do?

2. Is your organization aligned to support the game? Have all your major strategic decisions over a long time fitted consistently with the game you have chosen?

3. Given the overall evolution of your industry, what is the long-term sustainability of your game? When/how do you need to redirect or sharpen your focus to secure long-term growth and value creation?

4. Do you really understand the customer's needs for each specific customer segment? Have you designed your service delivery process to provide for these needs?

5. What is the core and unique strength of your business model and is this business model truly reflected in all the businesses in your current portfolio?

6. How is your business model replicable and what mechanisms do you have for transferring the business model into acquired or organically created units?

7. Which are the most important performance indicators for your company? How does each measure link to the central elements of the game you have picked and the business model that makes you uniquely positioned?

8. Do these key performance indicators play a central role in performance management processes (e.g. business planning, performance reviews, monthly reporting, incentive schemes) on all management levels of your company?

4

Leadership at the heart

What would have happened if Pierre Bellon, Thomas Berglund, Francis Mackay, J. Philip-Sørensen, Lars Nørby Johansen and their teams had not been running Sodexho, Securitas, Compass Group and Group 4 Falck for as long as they have? Would the four companies be the world leaders they are today? The answer lies in the realm of speculation. One of their industry peers had this to say:

> It certainly is an interesting phenomenon. You have to step back, try to understand how much of the dynamics of growth and valuation is related to a few personal leaders with vision, and how much of it relates to the dynamics of either markets or cultures. Executives who have come up through the business (this is especially true in a service business) know the business. They can't be fooled. I think that is so important, especially as the business gets bigger. The downside is that sometimes those executives are caught in the paradigms of the past, and they can't make the necessary changes according to the market's needs.
>
> Bill Pollard, Chairman, Service Master

We asked the same question of the five leaders. They attributed their success primarily to their teams of outstanding managers and legions of committed workers. They believe *anyone* with enough courage and will-power can make the difference. Take Securitas, for instance. The management team created the simple, wooden figure shown in Figure 4.1.

This diminutive icon stands in every branch manager's office – everybody at Securitas knows it – and represents understanding, commitment, keep it simple and set the example. These are the four

Figure 4.1

traits the company expects from its employees. As such, the little wooden figure is a model of one of the company's main principles – *you make the difference* – and although the four companies claim different values, it could embody one of the central values of all four companies: **people** *make the difference*. This is no surprise: in the security and food services industries, there are few tangible products, and if they do exist (like food ingredients or alarm systems) company success depends on how employees serve or handle them. The four companies in *Winning at Services: Lessons from Service Leaders* depend on the quality and values of the people who deliver their services, be it guards, chefs, waitresses, drivers or receptionists.

Compass Group, Group 4 Falck, Securitas and Sodexho all believe that role modelling (setting the example and living the values) is the best way to inspire their people and ensure that their hundreds of thousands of employees live the company values at their thousands of sites. John Dueholm puts a premium on visibility in management and leadership:

> *Visibility is vital, but also the demonstration of what leadership is and what the limits are. We have examples of people who have performed well in terms of result; however, they do not fit in our culture. These people leave, just as those who under-perform must leave. You have to understand the culture, and use your organization actively to create value.*
>
> John Dueholm, former COO of Group 4 Falck
> and as of 1 September 2002,
> Executive Vice President SAS, Scandinavian Airline Systems

Role modelling, our companies believe, is the way to improve their people-intensive services. Bellon, Berglund, Mackay, Nørby Johansen and Sørensen *choose* to serve as role models. They expect the same of their managers. All the leaders in the four companies inspire their people and show them the company service values by modelling those values themselves and they have done so consistently for many years.

> *You don't command people to give good service, you inspire people to give good service.*
>
> J. Philip-Sørensen, Chairman of the Board of Directors, Group 4 Falck

The five leaders would seem to follow the old maxim: do what I do. They believe that, given the right model, people can learn, and will learn, and that people, given half a chance, want to do a great job. In food service and security service, their behaviour seems to imply, company success depends on how individuals perform, and the leader's role is to be and act the way they expect their employees to be and to act. The way the leader treats his team members will be the way they treat their direct reports. If Securitas managers, for example, live and work by understanding, courage and commitment, and if they set an example inside the company, then front-line staff will serve Securitas customers with the same values. In other words, the way to inspire your employees is to be an inspiring leader.

Set a good example. Not by writing a handbook, but by living through things together with your people, creating understanding and a culture without too much talk. Show your people that you expect them to do as you do. If you want them to work hard, arrive early and leave late. If you want them to cooperate, leave your door open. If you want them to care about the figures, show them that you care. If you want your people to understand that developing people in organizations is important, do the training yourself. . . . Being a good example is ninety percent of all the management theory you'll ever need.

Securitas Toolbox booklet, page 39

In our interviews all leaders repeatedly made the point that one person at the top cannot make a difference in a service industry. Teamwork fuels company success. To build teamwork, they respect every person who works in their company, regardless of where that person rests in the company hierarchy. All leaders see their employees, not only as a prerequisite for success or a factor of production, but also as members of a 'loved' family.

It's not different running a company from having a family, bringing up your kids. They do what you do yourself not what you tell them to do. It's very difficult and very easy. Just by being a good example takes you 80% of the way in managing.

Thomas Berglund, CEO, Securitas

For these reasons, we say that Compass Group, Group 4 Falck, Securitas and Sodexho have 'leadership at the heart'. Because the top people are the heartbeats of their companies, they expect their regional, branch or site managers to be the heartbeat of a region, branch or site. They spend much more of their time and energy with their managers and front-line employees than do most CEOs or Chairmen. Despite setbacks and struggles, they have in them a conviction to something far greater than themselves, bigger than their own success. And they persist in any way they can, even at great personal expense.

Compass Group, Group 4 Falck, Securitas and Sodexho have created a constellation of forces – clear direction, the right people, simple and clear systems, processes, models, etc. – that flow from their values and serve as vehicles for them. How do these values manifest themselves in our five leaders and their companies? What characteristics do they share?

- The five leaders are **visionary industry shapers**. As such, they have framed a vision of the future, not only of their company but also its industry. To them, both the food services industry and the security industry offer many opportunities for development. They have created new professions. They set clear, unambiguous directions for their companies, and they have secured the wage, insurance, training, development and legislative fundamentals for their people to succeed.

- The four companies have **passionate and inspirational leaders**. Passion for and dedication to their companies run like a deep current underneath everything they do. They take time for their people, and aim to be accessible and visible – to everyone. They take the blame and give the credit liberally. Bellon, Berglund, Mackay, Nørby Johansen and Sørensen may lack the charisma or allure of a Forbes cover executive, but each has amassed a legion of inspired, loyal employees doing sometimes dangerous or get-down-dirty work for millions of customers.

- They are true **entrepreneurs**, no matter how you define the word; even as their companies took on the trimmings of large corporations, they took every reasonable chance to launch new ventures, grow organically or by acquisition. None of them worried first about his career; from day one, each focused on *getting the job done*. They manage by the conviction that effective leaders must, to slightly adapt John F. Kennedy's 1961 inaugural address, ask not what their company can do for them...ask what they can do for their company.

- All five have an unusually **intimate business knowledge** that comes from long tenures – ranging from 15 to 40 years – and assume responsibility for the minutest detail if required to do so.

Visionary industry shapers

A government can never force an industry to become good. It has to be led and improved by the industry itself...We think it's important not only to run your own company but also to some extent to take responsibility for what happens with the whole industry; to set standards, raise wages, work together with the unions. We, for example, have to have good relations with the police.

Thomas Berglund, CEO, Securitas

Senior managers in all four companies will tell you that raising standards – in service quality, safety, training, wages, and insurance and other benefits – is vital, not only in their companies, but, just as importantly, in their industries. Why? Because people are the basis for gaining and retaining clients, and improving customer and client satisfaction. To get good people, the industry must become more attractive. They have succeeded in making more professional some sectors of our economy that were for years regarded, fairly or not, as low-skill, low-wage, low-status, dangerous for the health of clients and workers (think of food poisoning scandals) and sometimes even on the edges of the law (think of corruption among security workers and shoot-outs involving cash-in-transit personnel).

Provide a vision for the long term

One of the key contributions that the company leaders and their teams have made to the success of the companies has been to formulate very simple visions and to stick to them for a very long time. Many CEOs have great visions, but few stick with them for more than a few years.

> Bellon had this vision of a global company and I remember that, maybe a year after I joined, he offered me a chance to buy shares in the company. It was private and unlisted, at a price I thought was fair. Bellon said the company would grow and be profitable, and I would enjoy the opportunity. And he was totally sure of that, he was sincere and he proved to be right. That was his vision and there was no doubt he would succeed.
>
> Patrice Douce, retired COO, Sodexho Alliance

The leaders in this book have a vision or dream. From it, they set the company's direction and carry it through. They seem to go by the mantra: *if you can dream it, you can make it.* They observe change around them, anticipate opportunity.

> Our view was that one of the leaders was going to consolidate the industry. It could be us, because of our track record . . . [besides], when I looked at the catering industry worldwide, the opportunities were limitless!
>
> Francis Mackay, Chairman, Compass Group

As described in Chapter 3, the leaders will tell you that you cannot run a successful service company unless you and your people know what the company can be best at, what it can do and can't do, and where it can compete to win. According to Mel Stark, a Hay Group consultant, one of the reasons Sodexho Alliance became one of the Forbes Most Admired companies in 1997 was the same reason that all companies on the most admired list earned their rank: they are more successful at translating their vision into reality. 'There is unanimity not only on goals, but also on where the company stands relative to those goals.'

SODEXHO

Mission: Improve the quality of everyday life.

Objective: To be, for all our clients, the benchmark wherever we offer our services, in every country, in every region, in every city.

Core values: Service spirit, team spirit and the spirit of progress.

When Pierre Bellon first started his catering business in Marseilles, small mom and pop shops like his met everyone's catering needs. But on a trip to the United States, he met the leader of Ara (now Aramark) and saw the tremendous potential for his modest business. However, he never dreamt that Sodexho would, 40 years later, be a world leader in food and management services.

Despite the fact that none of the leaders in this book ever anticipated the current size of their companies, the basic ideas in their visions were established decades earlier.

SECURITAS

Vision: To be a world leader in security.

Mission: Through our security work, we want to contribute towards a secure everyday life – to protect homes, workplaces and community. The three red dots in our logo remind us in our daily work of our basic values: Integrity, Vigilance and Helpfulness, which are, and will continue to be, the foundation of Securitas operations.

Although all five have distinct visions, they have all focused on better services – more reliable, more trustworthy – at the right price. Securitas refuses to do business with customers who want only the lowest price. The company is willing to forgo business if it will undermine the company's vision for a better security industry. Tony Sabatino, Area Manager of Securitas USA, notes that the company is sometimes forced to let go of clients:

> Some clients understand what we are trying to do; others see guards as a commodity. If after exhausting negotiations with a client we have to conclude that the client has different values and different objectives than us, at some point in time it makes sense to move forward and assign our employees elsewhere. It is important to keep clients, but it is also important not to sacrifice our values and vision.
>
> Tony Sabatino, Area Manager, Securitas

All four companies' true north has played a central role in their national and international expansion. This was already true at Compass Group in the early 1990s:

> At a strategy meeting of our top 20 managers in 1991, I laid out a vision of where we would actually be in five years time, in terms of being present in the US, present in Europe, and present in Scandinavia and Asia. And I remember that they were completely thrown by the vision, that here we were, a 250 million pound business, and I was saying, 'In five years' time we will have a turnover of 2.5 billion pounds.
>
> Francis Mackay, Chairman, Compass Group

More than once, Francis Mackay has faced withering personal criticism over what he felt was right for the company. When Mackay and his team announced Compass Group's first big American acquisition, the £300 million purchase of Canteen, in 1994, financial analysts were sceptical and shareholders were furious. Shareholders argued that the company should stay out of the US market, which had proved problematic for many British companies. The press was as negative as the shareholders, but Mackay weathered the storm and the deal was a success. Consider the controversial £17.5 billion merger of Compass Group with Granada in May 2001. Mackay's shareholders accused him of jeopardizing 10 years of spectacular growth by taking on a huge hotel portfolio that sat awkwardly alongside its existing business. But Mackay stuck to his visionary guns, went on with the deal, promised his shareholders this was the best option for Compass Group (he would sell the hotel business later) and – as the figures testify – was true to his words. By mid-2001 the company had become virtually debt free, which enabled it to go for further large acquisitions in the food services industry.

COMPASS GROUP

Vision/goal: To be the highest quality and most profitable owner and operator of the world's top food service and hospitality business. Compass Group's vision is based on a strategic focus in five key areas: Customer and client satisfaction; Market leadership; Preferred employer; Operational excellence; Financial performance.

Mission: To achieve leadership in our chosen food service markets through the constant pursuit, in association with our clients and partners, of superior levels of service, efficiency and quality.

The five leaders admit that they didn't start their business lives as visionaries. When their companies were small, or when they first started in the leader job, they had no explicit vision for becoming the biggest or the number one in anything.

When I became the leader of Compass Group [1991], I did not immediately have the vision of becoming a world leader in food services, but I did within the first six months. I realized that we needed to really get a grip on the catering business.
                                    Francis Mackay, Chairman, Compass Group

GROUP 4 FALCK

Vision: To become the leading global provider of security and security-related services. The term 'leading' is defined as a combination of being among the very largest in the global market, and providing the best quality of services to customers.

Mission: To provide assistance to people, authorities and companies in order to meet their demand for safety and security as individuals or groups on an everyday basis. Group 4 Falck views its most important task as the further development of the Group's special core competencies within security, safety and global solutions, in order to ensure that customers, as well as national and international communities, always see the Group as a leading professional, responsible and reliable operator.

Raise standards in the industry

In the late 1990s and early 2000s, the status of jobs in food services and security has risen from 'something anyone can do with some hours of training' to a true profession. Securitas, by working on many industry fronts, tries to enact legislation, raise wages and improve training for staff. Group 4 Falck pushes legislation in the United Kingdom and elsewhere. Sodexho and Compass Group make no compromises on quality or food safety. Let's take a look at what Securitas says to its more than 2000 branch managers.

> *Why on earth should we develop the industry? To develop your business, it's vital that you influence the factors that currently limit your operations – governments make laws for security companies, the police issue regulations, standards are set by legislation or by the industry on both training and security issues, customer organizations develop their views and expectations, employees and their organizations have their opinions. By living close to our 'partners' in the security environment we help set the industry standards and create a working environment in which we can grow. The single most important factor in creating good service in a security company is having good people who develop and grow with us. In many countries, the type of services we provide are still perceived as low prestige. We are going to change that. Providing good services requires good people, trained people. Recruiting people means paying decent wages . . . [here] we are dependent on influencing the whole industry.*
>
> Securitas Toolbox booklet page 29

Almost everything Securitas publishes or does goes back to the company's aim to improve the standards of security work, both for clients and for staff. After the 11 September 2001 attacks on the World Trade Center and Pentagon, Securitas, as the quote from CNN below illustrates, had even more of a willing ear for its pledge to improve the guarding industry:

> *The Federal Aviation Administration is about to set new certification standards for airport security companies. Airlines, responsible for staffing security checkpoints, contract the work out to the other companies, keeping an eye on their bottom line . . . they routinely take the lowest bidder. [. . .] Security screeners at many airports often make less money than fast-food workers in the terminals, leading to high turnover rate at some facilities. The GAO (General Accounting Office), for*

example, found that the St. Louis airport had a 400% turnover in security
screeners in the fiscal year ending April 1999. The airport in Atlanta, Georgia had
a 375% turnover in the same period. By comparison . . . the annual turnover rate
at Belgium's airport is 5%; at Manchester, England it is 1%. The difference . . . :
higher wages and better insurance.

CNN.com/US Edition 18 September 2001

The goal? Convince everyone that corporate and personal safety is worth the price. Turn the industry from one dominated by lowest-bidder-takes-all contracting to one in which companies are willing to pay the right price for better quality. This can be quite a challenge, since security, especially in the United States, has had a reputation for paying low wages for long hours to shady characters with a cold gaze, large biceps, and a criminal record. The US market is very price-driven and competitive; Securitas' management is people-driven, and focused on mutual success and sharing of benefits. Of course, raising standards is also about raising profits, but even more about doing the right thing for all parties involved: customers, employees and shareholders.

In the decade and a half before the turn of the century, Securitas saw this approach work in Europe, where it upped the quality of services delivered by paying higher wages forged in union talks and, incidentally, improved working conditions, and profits, too. Consider what happened in Spain. The private security industry started in Spain in the 1970s after dramatic and sweeping political and social turbulence. Like many other countries, crime, or rather the fear of crime, was on the increase, and the increased prosperity of the population as well as increasing technical and financial complexity was starting to lead to greater vulnerability for companies, organizations and individuals. During the 1980s industry growth was rapid and uncontrolled. Price wars, low pay scales, a poor working environment, low profitability and low-quality services were fuelling the fires of conflict. In 1992, with the acquisition of Esabe, Securitas took on the challenge of nursing the sick security industry patient in Spain back to health. Unions and employers had traditionally been at each other's throats, but in an important first step, the company, in constant, wearisome dialogue with the unions, raised wages by 20% between 1997 and 2001. The response from one of Spain's largest unions?

'It was proof...that we struggle jointly to eradicate the stigma attached to the industry and see that agreements are observed.' To get more forceful legislation in place, the company started discussions with the police and the Ministry of the Interior.

Long ago, Securitas' top management made a 'lifetime commitment to the industry', which means: take responsibility for setting standards and raising wages, rules for training (some countries require 400 hours of guard training, while others require nothing), pushing legislation that keeps unwanted elements out of the industry, working in partnership with the unions, cementing good relations with the police and governmental authorities, rationalizing guarding services with electronics across the industry to improve service and pass higher prices on to employees in higher wages, and training customers to understand the business, recognize and appreciate good business. But Securitas is not alone.

Andrew Stern is President of SEIU (Service Employees International Union), the largest union in the United States. SEIU's mission is 'to change the lives of working Americans especially in the service sector'. Stern got to know Securitas as part of his SEIU work with counterpart unions in Europe. He remembers his first encounter with Securitas at a 1998 service workers conference in Europe:

> *Thomas Berglund of Securitas gave a presentation on the company and its strategic plans. It was so fundamentally different from anything that we'd ever heard from an American company that we – the American delegates – all found it hard to believe. In the United States the objective in the sector was to compete on a low-wage basis, to underbid the competition, and to worry – less about the long term – but just about the next quarter and the report to the stock market. Securitas aimed for higher wages, low turnover and development of its staff. With a high-quality, stable workforce, it takes care of long-term return to shareholders. When I first heard this I thought I had gone to heaven!*
>
> *Securitas has a tough job in the States, I think they want to continue to follow this strategy but they have inherited many American managers, who think the European management is living in dreamland, because it really is going to require a semi-revolution of how the industry operates in the United States. But then again, all of their American managers understand that the reason they are now part of Securitas is that the company has been so successful.*
>
> *Andrew Stern, President, SEIU, USA*

Sørensen and Nørby Johansen of Group 4 Falck have made the same commitment. Nørby Johansen describes the responsibilities of a security industry leader as:

> *Our industry is a low margin, low-reputation industry in which we hire mostly unskilled labour. It is therefore one of our most important jobs to develop that industry. We have an obligation to form trade associations, to set standards, to formulate terms and conditions and to make sure that the people in our industry are better trained and get more competencies.*
>
> Lars Nørby Johansen, CEO, Group 4 Falck

Between 1962 and 1996, Group 4 Belgian crews suffered three deaths at the hands of armed attackers. Two of the killings happened between 1994 and 1996, when raids were shocking the CIT (cash in transit) sector in Belgium once a week. Several Group 4 men were badly injured in related shootings. Not content to ride their cash trucks like silent targets, all of the industry's CIT crews went on strike for six weeks from February to March 1998. Group 4 made an agreement with the unions that a third man should be added to the two-man crews. The company, which was already plugged into an R&D programme, came up with a technical answer: the 'IQ SEC container', an intelligent security device that bores holes in the bank notes inside as soon as the attackers tinker with the cash box. The unions welcomed IC SEC's approval and introduction, and agreed to a return to two-man crews. This union support was essential for Group 4, since it was not economically viable to operate three-man crews as well as the IQ SEC, which had required a huge investment in time and capital. Group 4 has not kept this life-saving device for itself, it has made the IQ SEC available to all security companies.

For Securitas and Group 4 Falck, running the industry includes far more than directly improving the guard or CIT crew members' jobs: it also includes getting legislation in place to regulate the security industry. If Berglund has his numbers right (1998), 'In the United Kingdom, police estimated that up to 3000 employees in security companies are more or less criminal people.' According to *Securitas Magazine* (January 2002), the legislation that rules the private security industry differs greatly between countries and states. For example, in Alabama, USA, at the time of writing, a security officer could theoretically be hired at 2 p.m. and be out on the streets for the 6 o'clock shift, without any training or background checks carried out. In Sweden, on the other hand, the guard's profession is subject to rigorous legislation and official controls. Guards are also screened before they are hired and are required to undergo extensive training before they start.

As early as 1971, Sørensen of Group 4 Falck initiated a campaign for the licensing of the UK private security industry and, in 2001, saw his ambition realized with the Private Security Industry Bill getting Royal Assent. With the new law, everybody working in security in the United Kingdom is required to have a licence and no criminal record. Securitas, ever the standard-bearer, feels that the law should be even stronger, covering training and quality, too. After all, Swedish law requires 217 hours of mandatory training, comprising 81 hours of theory and 136 hours of practice, with an examination following. As agreed by the industry, all guards get an additional two days of training every year, and specialized training programmes are available. Local police authorities run a background check, and the applicant must have a clean record.

Sørensen also initiated the entry of the private security industry in public/private partnerships such as managing Her Majesty's Prisons in the United Kingdom, activities that now operate under Group 4 Falck Global Solutions Limited. As of 2001, Berglund was still optimistic that there would be considerable progress on standards in the five years to come. Group 4 Falck, which in March 2002 acquired the second largest security services provider in the United States, Wackenhut, shares the Securitas views on standards:

> *Our vision is to professionalize the industry. We can never be better than the guards we employ.*
>
> Lars Nørby Johansen, CEO, Group 4 Falck

Securitas launched its Group Council in 1997 to provide what the company calls a 'cross border information forum' with a brief to discuss matters pertinent to employees. Every country where Securitas operates is invited to provide union representation on the Council, whose annual meetings are also attended by Thomas Berglund and Amund Skarholt, deputy CEO and President Security Services USA, respectively, and Hakan Winberg, Chief Financial Officer. One of the main, stated objectives of the Group Council was to ensure that unions and management work alongside each other. The information exchanged at Group meetings helps the members from a wide array of countries learn how to work with their local unions more effectively, as partners. Typical concerns are raising the quality and value of services, improving relations with society at large, authorities, employees and union organizations, and creating conditions for developing the company's services and the industry as a whole. Every time Securitas moves into a new country, it invites representatives to the Group Council and, where necessary, even pays for their English lessons. Member countries include, for example, Austria, France, Norway, Finland, Sweden, Denmark, the United Kingdom, Spain, Switzerland, Germany and the United States.

Just as in the security industry, players like Sodexho and Compass are doing their best to raise the standards in the food service industry all around the world. Hans Rijnierse, Managing Director of Sodexho, Netherlands testifies that Sodexho encourages its managers to influence industry standards in their own countries. Like Pierre Bellon, Rijnierse is active on the board of an employers' association (VNO-NCW, the largest in The Netherlands). He represents the Dutch service industry on the board and spends almost 30% of his time on improving the standards in the service industry, talking with politicians, meeting about legislation, social dialogue, etc.:

> Catering used to be a low-image business in The Netherlands, but not any more. We have managed to gain respect for what we do. We work with our social partners – like the unions. But the main responsibility for improving the standards in business services lies with the employers and the employers' association.
>
> Hans Rijnierse, Managing Director, Sodexho The Netherlands
> and Deputy Chairman Sodexho South Africa

Faced with an image that is not yet markedly different from other food and management services companies, in 2000, Sodexho decided to affirm its new strategic vision and shift its approach to the market to reflect its concern for raising standards and improving image. The new strategic vision strives to strengthen the company's competitive position by driving faster organic growth and increasing the responsibilities of its 'Worldwide Market Champions'. The company wants to achieve this organic growth by:

1. segmenting and sub-segmenting its client base to enhance client and customer satisfaction;
2. broadening its food services offer to include vending, room service, take-out sales, directors' tables and prestige dining; and
3. developing other strategies, e.g. ground maintenance, conference room management, technical maintenance of buildings and equipment, sterilization of surgical instruments, and tutoring.

These three strategies, and the activities that support them, add up to fighting what Sodexho now calls 'the battle for value for [its] clients'. Sodexho has chosen to fight this 'battle' because of two weighty features of its core business. First, people generally don't have a very high opinion of the industry, which they perceive to be little more than providing commodity services. And second, according to the Chairman's February 2002 Report to the Annual Shareholders' Meeting, Sodexho 'enjoys no clear differentiation with regard to its competitors'. The trend, at the turn of the millennium, among some of Sodexho's large international corporate clients, was to put contracts out to bid and assign negotiations to price-driven purchasing departments. The result? A high risk of underpaid staff with diminishing skills and uninspiring, increasingly low value-added services. In its education and healthcare segments, Sodexho faces the same pressures: local officials and authorities see their duty as negotiating services for the *lowest possible* price. But the drawbacks are clear. Consider the recent public outcry in Europe about food scares:

> *We refuse to increase market share by bidding so low we can't deliver high quality services. Bear in mind that our net margin is currently below 2% of revenues. We also refuse to expand by offering commodity services, because our mission is to 'improve the quality of daily life' for every child, student, employee, patient or senior in every establishment we serve.*
>
> Pierre Bellon, Chairman, Sodexho Alliance

So how does Sodexho try to create value for its clients (and lead the industry along the way)? The answer is by improving its clients' productivity – by helping clients use their sites more efficiently and more productively. In the United Kingdom, for example, reception facilities at Royal Ascot Racecourse are rented for conventions, conferences and gala evenings. Sodexho also helps to make the clients' employee more efficient and productive. The customers who live and work at the facilities Sodexho manages want their daily lives made more pleasant in every way possible: they want to eat well, get the best value for money, live or work in a nice environment, with spaces where they can relax or have fun. So Sodexho has created a shop on clients' premises that makes office employees' work and personal lives more convenient with various services like dry cleaning and car maintenance. Lastly, Sodexho works to improve the image and reputation of its clients by making their establishments more attractive in the eyes of their customers and other users. An ambitious programme of buildings, grounds and services improvement at Loyola University (USA) is a top example.

In November 1999, to lead the way toward verifiable food safety across the industry, Sodexho set up a consultative group of scientific specialists. The company, as a 'leading food service provider for organizations of all kinds', sees itself at the 'heart of public health concerns'. The consultative body works to ensure legislative and scientific vigilance, and enables Sodexho to have ongoing assessments of the food industry so it can alert its operations whenever threats arise. The experts advise on food safety procedures, new staff programmes and new supply chains that ensure food safety. The company, in its steadfast commitment to food safety keeps a wakeful eye on genetically modified (GM) foods. Sodexho will not use GM products of any kind. In the meat supply chain, the company will only approve suppliers who guarantee a rigorous observance of strict hygiene and food safety regulations.

Beyond safety issues, the company also works to lead the industry in other ways. It wants to set the benchmark in its business, and is always looking to improve its understanding of client requirements, and the evolving behaviour, needs and values of its customers. How? Through the Sodexho Research Institute on the Quality of Daily Life, various customer research programmes, Conviv'Styles, a biennial School Meals Survey in the United Kingdom, and customer profiling in the United Kingdom. Since 1999, the Sodexho Institute on the Quality of Life has represented what the company calls 'a unique, global initiative that adds credibility to the group's position'. The Institute has already published three studies on topics relating to the quality of everyday life. To complement the more common qualitative and quantitative research techniques, it has formed partnerships with international organizations such as the UN, UNESCO, and the WHO to collect and study data, and has already published two research papers on topics relating to the quality of everyday life.

Passionate and inspirational leaders

Set the example

Leadership is about setting a good example and getting employees involved. This is how a good working environment is created, with opportunities for employees to develop and grow.

Securitas literature

From the light joking and jollity of J. Philip-Sørensen, to the modest 'lucky' Francis Mackay, to the quiet, almost self-deprecating determination of Thomas Berglund, to the mercurial tantrums of strategist Pierre Bellon, to the buoyant Lars Nørby Johansen, all five leaders, by virtue of character and action, set the example, flavour the company culture, influence policy and shape values. Who they are and what they do is intertwined, and the companies reflect their characters and their values. All five, in their own ways, care about people, love service and get satisfaction from giving their people space to work and seeing them succeed; their warmth is genuine. They seek these same qualities in their managers, too. They and their managers do stints on the front line: at Securitas, for example, a branch or district manager who has never been a guard, regularly fills in for guards on the job to know how guards feel, to get to the end of a night shift at 6 a.m. and greet the first factory workers cheerfully.

People describe Berglund as 'calm' and a 'visionary', an 'ambitious and focused' man with 'a human touch'. Management, according to Berglund, is based on managers setting a good example for their employees, or, as company literature describes it, 'by acting responsibly, employees show their colleagues how they, too, should act'. Sørensen, or JPS as his colleagues know him, believes that whatever you do, it must be fun. 'The day the circus goes out of the office is the day the office dies.' He has a knack of putting people at ease, and, during his visits to Group 4 Falck offices or customer sites, makes time to talk to individuals at all levels, often surprising them by remembering personal details from their last conversation. One of his credos is to always remain calm: 'You have to walk, keep cool, handle things in a logical manner, don't get excited. . . . When a Roman Senator runs across the square you know you are in trouble!'

Mackay – 'Francis' to most of his colleagues – loves people, from the man who runs the elevator to the manager colleague. During his visit to IMD, he had a conversation in French – maybe not grammatically correct, but very amicable – with the chef about running the kitchen for a demanding client such as IMD. Mackay, say those who work with him, 'brings an incredible calm and determination to projects he cares about'. He is unruffled, confident and tolerant under pressure – a genuinely nice, humble person who goes out of his way to be on the best terms with everyone, whether they are the most senior or the most junior person on the staff. Mackay knows the difference between information, and information that matters. He stands back and turns a decision in his mind. He knows the details but he's no controller. He has a subtle wit, free from sarcastic notes. Most strangers would probably find it hard not to warm to his booming rumble of a laugh. Mackay has consciously chosen some of these managerial traits:

I worked for many different people, and the ones that I really didn't like working for were the ones that you never quite knew where you were with them. One day they were really friendly and very kind, and another day they seemed to have gone mad. I realized that was not the sort of environment that people like to work in. So I try to keep a very balanced approach to problems – crises and success – and treat it all very much the same. So calmness is important . . . and friendliness I think is another

*one. I like people, and I like people whether they are operating the lift or whether
they are the Chief Executive.*

Francis Mackay, Chairman, Compass Group

Bellon – 'Monsieur Pierre Bellon', to most people who work with him,
with the French formal 'vous' – has an almost uncanny knack for strategy,
picking the right people and setting them off in the right direction. A
retired vice president of the company recalls that Bellon would not eat in
any Sodexho restaurant without shaking the chef's or the head waiter's
hand, and he manages to do it naturally, without any obsequy. Hans
Rijnierse, Managing Director, recounts how, the first year he worked with
Bellon, from time to time they met for reporting and to share concerns. At
one such meeting, Bellon outlined the myriad problems he saw in The
Netherlands. Rijnierse disagreed. Bellon, who was not accustomed to such
open disagreement, 'leaped out of his chair'. But at the end of the day,
Bellon walked him to the taxi and said, 'You know, we are friends again.'
This warm, personal gesture, notes Rijnierse, set the tone for his later
successful work with Bellon.

Bellon serves as a role model and expects his people at all levels to do the
same. At the same time, he looks for his own role models:

*I have learned from others who had more experience than me. And today I tell my
managers, we are incompetent. Why? Because we have never managed a company
of this size. So what should we do? We look at companies who are even larger than
we are and we learn from them how to manage on a large international scale.*

Pierre Bellon, Chairman, Sodexho Alliance

Live the values

*I have always believed that the growth of Sodexho is directly related to the courage,
the will and the competency of those who manage it.*

Pierre Bellon, Chairman, Sodexho Alliance

The leaders manage by simple strong values on which they will not
compromise. And these values, whatever they may be or however the
companies describe them – helpfulness, respect, vigilance, team spirit –

define the characters of the companies: the no-nonsense clarity of Securitas, the courage of Group 4 Falck, the modest and purposeful team play of Compass Group, the enjoyment in improving the quality of life of Sodexho. The companies' spirits mirror the leaders' values. Although their values differ, the four companies have applied their values over many years. They dedicate themselves to making sure all the people in their companies understand them and make them their own. They reinforce these values over and over, from the core outward to the last person at the most distant site, like a ripple in a pond. Let's have a closer look.

Securitas values: Integrity, vigilance, helpfulness

> *Why are we here? Because we are driven by duty, joy and passion. The duty to use the resources we have inside ourselves to contribute to the good forces in life. The joy that doing this creates in ourselves and others. The passion for achieving more, showing what is possible, challenging the heights . . . at Securitas we have learned the hard way to focus on value.*
>
> *Securitas Toolbox booklet*

How did Securitas learn the hard way that values matter? The company had guards who were stealing from customers. One such incident has been analysed to the bone and has been turned into management training material. Reality-based training efforts like this must make sure that every Securitas employee adheres to the values they wear on their sleeves: the three red dots that stand for *integrity, vigilance* and *helpfulness*.

1. *Integrity*: Securitas 'never compromises in its demand for truthfulness'. It expects its employees to be honest, and trustworthy to work unsupervised on customers' premises and with valuables. According to Chantal Austin, Regional Manager Securitas Normandy France, 'the main difference between us and our competitors is ethics, both with our customers and our staff. We never promise anything we cannot deliver, and we never sell customers a service they do not need.' The company encourages employees to express their opinions, never withholding information and always reporting improprieties.

2. *Vigilance*: For Securitas, professionalism means seeing, hearing and evaluating – guards are always attentive. Professional vigilance means guards developing an intuition that helps them see things others don't, which is necessary in order to stay aware of potential risks or untoward incidents on the premises of a customer.

3. *Helpfulness*: As part of a general push to make life safer, the company expects its people to assist, even when helping is unrelated to their jobs. Again Chantal Austin: 'Guards often work when a factory is closed, and see things at night the owners don't see when they're working. Employees may leave emergency doors open to facilitate theft. We sometimes have to say things to a customer he doesn't want to hear, and this is part of our integrity and helpfulness.'

'The Securitas 20 theses', a basic values document for the more than 230 000 people who give the company a face, reflect the company's customer orientation.

BASIC VALUES FOR SECURITAS EMPLOYEES: 20 THESES

1. Our task, as Securitas employees, is to prevent and limit damage that may deprive our fellow men of their work, and otherwise cause harm to life, health and property. Everyone within Securitas works towards this goal, and hence we must all do our job to the best of our ability.

2. A Securitas employee has integrity – that is why customers trust us to work unsupervised on their premises.

3. A Securitas employee is vigilant – our professionalism involves, *inter alia*, seeing, hearing and evaluating.

4. A Securitas employee is helpful – we help out when necessary, even if it is not part of our job.

5. A Securitas employee has a sense of responsibility – what you have been entrusted with may constitute a temptation but when you live up to that trust, you gain self-confidence.

6. Being a Securitas employee means we have accepted an obligation to report the defects, irregularities and deficiencies we discover – even when they apply to a colleague.

7. A Securitas employee never compromises his/her duty to report.

8. When someone has done something wrong, or made a mistake that must be corrected, this should be done in a way that cannot be experienced as demeaning or insulting.
9. When writing reports, ask yourself, 'Can this report make a constructive contribution to the activities of the customer or the person to whom it relates?'
10. As Securitas employees, we have accepted a professional secrecy obligation. This is designed to protect you, Securitas, and our customers.
11. A Securitas employee regards every misappropriation of other people's property as theft, irrespective of value.
12. It is part of the operations management's duties to make clear to their co-workers what preconditions and limitations apply to the conduct of their work.
13. A Securitas employee never takes bribes – perks and presents can be exploited by the giver or hide potentially harmful intentions.
14. A Securitas employee never allows him or herself to become dependent – if you are, your ability to carry out your job correctly can be restricted.
15. A Securitas employee behaves in a way that ensures he/she sets a good example, whether on duty or off. His/her professionalism is also judged on his/her private behaviour and lifestyle.
16. The Securitas employee is visible – criticism of an individual employee reflects badly on everyone.
17. Within Securitas we strive to achieve confidence in each other. By showing confidence in someone you gain their confidence in you.
18. Openness and truthfulness are a prerequisite of trust within Securitas.
19. Appreciation and attentiveness breed self-confidence – self-confidence can be gained by showing appreciation and attentiveness.
20. It is part of every Securitas employee's responsibility to help and teach new colleagues, not only in terms of their work, but in terms of our ethical and moral principles.

Group 4 Falck: Honesty, alertness, helpfulness

At the end of a day of guarding the only thing you can take with you is the dirt on the soles of your shoes.

Philip Sørensen, grandfather of J. Philip-Sørensen

Group 4 Falck, with the same roots as rival Securitas, follows much the same values: honesty, alertness, and helpfulness. J. Philip-Sørensen, member of the third Sørensen generation in the security industry, echoes the high moral standards his father and grandfather set in the early days. Every Group 4 Falck management employee signs the Group's Code of Ethics and Conflict of Interest Statement, a rather complex, legalistic document that emphasizes integrity and sets out the ethical values to which all must adhere. The Code of Conduct is also part of the induction training for new staff.

No values appear in the Group 4 Falck annual report, but every employee we spoke to claimed to know them. Lars Nørby Johansen, President and CEO, will tell you that it is the company's values (and only its values) that are international. They include ethics and customer orientation, giving customers more than they expect. Nels Petersen, Group Communications Director, who has been working at Group 4 Falck, with a two-and-a-half year hiatus, since 1985, suggests that, for the thousands of ambulance drivers, firemen and guards, the values translate into the idea that, regardless of company hierarchy, the company charges them to *take responsibility*, *act now*, and, *if in doubt, do the right thing*. How does the company communicate these values? 'The most obvious way', says Petersen, 'is role modelling'.

> *Consider the transportation of a patient, say, 'Mrs Nielsen'. Mrs Nielsen calls a taxi, the driver shows up, rolls down his window and tells her she can get in the back. Group 4 Falck employees get out of the car, go up, ring the door bell and take Mrs Nielsen under the arm, walk her out to the car and do the same when they get to the hospital, pick her up again, drive her home, and say, 'Can we do anything else to help you?'*
>
> *Nels Petersen, Director Group Communications, Group 4 Falck*

At Group 4 Falck being honest and helpful with the people you serve extends upward into management. Johnny Eikeland, employee representative on the Group board (previously a rescuer and now information officer), says this includes CEO Lars Nørby Johansen, too:

> *Lars went on a road show to talk to the firefighters and the ambulance guys – about what his intentions were and why it was necessary to reorganize the business. He told them, 'Unfortunately, I have to fire two hundred of you to get the business up and running again. That is how it is. I am very sorry about it, but I am speaking openly with you and want to talk about how we can get through this.' The rescuers*

and firefighters all stood up and clapped and shouted 'Rah Rah Falck'. That is incredible.

Johnny Eikeland, Information Officer, Group 4 Falck

Compass Group: Setting values in each sector

We are committed to providing equal opportunities for all our people, actively encouraging equal employment, training and career development regardless of background. And our successful track record is based on a clear, consistent strategy for long-term growth and our focus on the key areas of client and customer satisfaction, market leadership, operational excellence, financial performance and being a preferred employer.

Compass Group Annual Report

Compass Group does not trumpet its values. But from the company's five-point mission statement – customer and client satisfaction, market leadership, preferred employer, operational excellence, financial performance – you can read what is important to the company. Peruse the description and you'll find phrases that reflect Compass Group's values: total dedication, reliability, commitment, genuine conviction (that how our service is delivered is just as important as what is delivered), putting the customer and client first, close working relationship, partnership, listen carefully, respond quickly, efficiency, quality, and people. In contrast to a company like Securitas, Compass Group lets each sector – business and industry, fine dining, specialist services, education, healthcare, travel/retail/ leisure, sports and events, vending – identify its own values and focus. Each determines the values it needs to meet the company's stated mission: to achieve leadership in its chosen food service markets through the constant pursuit, in association with its clients and partners, of superior levels of service, efficiency and quality.

Sodexho: Service spirit, team spirit, progress

True dignity lies in being of service to others. A team wins when its members, regardless of their diverse personalities, qualities and skills, respect and appreciate each other, deciding their strategy and tactics together, then putting their ideas into practice without anyone seeking any more credit than anyone else. Winning is the objective, but only when the members of the team put the group's interests before their own ambitions.

Pierre Bellon, Chairman, Sodexho Alliance

Take service spirit and team spirit, and mix them with progress, and you have the Sodexho values. According to Jean-Pierre Cuny, a retired Sodexho Division Manager, even if, while progressing, the company strategy evolves, Sodexho's vision always remains the same. Every Sodexho manager we spoke to mentioned the three values as an integral part of Sodexho's vision. At Sodexho, service spirit is an attitude towards daily life, a way of being. It is, as company information suggests, 'listening, paying attention to details, being available, responsive, welcoming and efficient'.

Sodexho Alliance describes the progress value as a 'spirit' that comes from the Japanese. The Japanese, one manager pointed out, believe that everybody who can do a job can also say how that job can be done better, quicker, cheaper and in a nicer way. This runs counter to a typical 'Western' service attitude: 'I'm not paid much, so I will do what you say and will not let you know how we could improve together.' Sodexho believes that the Japanese-like attitude sets the company apart – whenever managers respond negatively to new ideas or complain about too much work, there will be somebody to remind them of the Sodexho spirit of progress.

'Team spirit', notes the Sodexho annual report 'is as essential at [Sodexho] sites as it is in the boardroom.'

If you don't work as a team in our business, then nothing works. It's true in a kitchen: if the team isn't cohesive, it won't work, but even at higher levels, you need cross-fertilization of know-how, and that will fail if people are pursuing their own agendas.

Patrice Douce, retired COO, Sodexho Alliance

On loyalty and long-term commitment, Hans Rijnierse, one of Sodexho's country managers representing the Dutch business acquired in 1995, notes with a smile:

In the first year of the takeover at a meeting in Paris, things were getting a little tense. I explained to Pierre Bellon that Sodexho was the sixth owner in Van Hecke catering in 33 years, so that by now we'd seen plenty of structural change with each new owner. Bellon replied, 'It could be that we are the sixth, but more important for you to know is that we will be the last.'

Hans Rijnierse, Managing Director Sodexho The Netherlands
and Deputy Chairman Sodexho South Africa

Douce and Bellon believe that for the company to progress, every single individual on every team at every Sodexho site around the world must strive to give their best in what they call 'the spirit of service'. Says Douce, 'This is why we are so committed to innovation, improvement and anticipating the needs of clients and customers...the group's progress comes directly from the collective and personal progress of all its people.' If you want to go far at Sodexho, you have to go the extra mile, continuously improve performance, dare to take the initiative and question the daily routines.

The spirit of progress in a service business is an endless exercise. You are never there. The challenge we have is to repeat and improve. We see that expectations vary, and tomorrow should be better than today, so it's what I call a voyage. The spirit of service. In the service industry if we don't have this basic spirit, we should do something else. If at the highest levels people are not keen to serve others, there is a problem. I'll give you an example: in starting to serve clients, I have done some cooking. I had clients calling me, 'Patrice, your French fries are sloppy.' I would never say, 'Okay, call Mr or Mrs So-And-So.' I said, 'Tell me where it happened.' That's what I call the spirit of service.

Patrice Douce, retired COO, Sodexho Alliance

Staying in touch

How can a security guard in India know what Group 4 stands for? We've got 38 000 thousand guards in India so it's difficult for me personally to contact them all individually, but ... the answer is still: by being there. You can't send out a directive from headquarters saying, 'From tomorrow we're all going to behave like this.' It won't work. So you – the manager – have to be there, talk to them, visit them, even the smallest branch office ... that should be implanted into all levels of management. That's what they have to do. It's very simple. There's a large portion of common sense. Sadly, common sense today is a rather rare commodity.

J. Philip-Sørensen, Chairman of the Board of Directors, Group 4 Falck

Being in touch, talking to people – employees, customers, members of the industry, shareholders out in even the most remote parts of the world – are key values of the four companies. All top managers in the four companies live by the dictum that company success comes down to your spoken word, your behaviour and the power of your personality. Our five leaders are inveterate travellers, logging hundreds of thousands of frequent-flyer miles every year. They spend a significant amount of their time and energy with their managers *and* their front-line employees. They travel three or four days a week to visit operations: managers, employees, customers and shareholders. Bellon does four countries plus a trip to the United States every month, paying special attention to Sodexho's great performers and making sure to meet chefs, waiters, etc. J. Philip-Sørensen in the past and Lars Nørby Johansen today spend three days out of five visiting Group 4 Falck company sites. These visits to the different country organizations usually last three to four days each.

> I go out to each office, and even if the picture is not hanging straight on the wall I will adjust that to show that I am really with them. I am completely absorbed with the people there. My mobile is off. If I get a message from Head Office to say we've got problems, I'll ask the secretary to phone back to that office and say 'Solve it. I'm busy!' For every visit, I have small black boxes with me – Kazakhstan, India, Portugal, or whatever – and before I land in a country, I will have pulled out – say the Kazakh – box, and looked up the latest accounts, latest sales statistics, latest news, so when I meet these people I really know what I'm talking about.
> J. Philip-Sørensen, Chairman of the Board of Directors, Group 4 Falck

When Sørensen gets to a country, he has what he calls his 'programme':

> I say to the local managing director, 'If you want me to see customers, if you want me to travel around the country, if you want me to chair meetings – whatever you want me to do, I'll do it. But, don't give me long dinners and long lunches, unless it is for our own staff or customers. Don't give me a lot of claptrap with culture because I'll get that in my free time, if I have any. Let me be with the people. But, I don't want to sit in your office and you call people in, one by one, and sit in a queue outside to come in and say hello to the chairman.
> J. Philip-Sørensen, Chairman of the Board of Directors, Group 4 Falck

Linda Sharpe says that in the early days there was more to these visits:

> He knew everybody's birthdays, wives' names, children's birth dates. He went to every single board meeting, even when the company was expanding in the early

1990s . . . it didn't matter whether it was in Greece, Bulgaria, Turkey, Austria or Canada, and when the board meeting was over, he would go out and see something in operation, shake the hand of a guard; he rated the people on the front line. He believed that the guards were the ambassadors of the company, the most important element of our service delivery.

Linda Sharpe, Principal, Group 4 Falck Academy

Berglund also spends an inordinate amount of time meeting with people in the company and in the industry. This close monitoring and the heavy travel schedule required send a message to everybody in Securitas: the leader cares enough to want to know the details.

I basically travel every day, more or less. Some weeks it's six days; other weeks it's three or four days. But I would say, on average, it's four or five days a week. I do not spend much time at my head office. It has only 15 people to talk to so I go out and see the other 200 000 plus!

Thomas Berglund, CEO, Securitas

Every quarter he meets with investors and sometimes in between, too. He also spends a lot of time with different organizations in the industry 'also to know what to buy the next time [we do an acquisition]'. And then, of course, he follows up on the different divisions: 'I go through the different figures on my own, then I meet the managers every month to go through the numbers'.

One of the companies, Group 4 Falck, doesn't make use of an Investors Relations Department, which adds to its managers' burden of being accessible and visible. The leaders and members of the top team have contact with investors, taking calls and jetting the globe to give road shows to investors and potential investors. But they also travel, not just to visit sites, but to teach internally, running company workshops, conferences and training.

With a business in a hundred countries, it is important to get out. One of the things I introduced when I became chief executive was what I called 'walk the talk', where I would actually go to a country for three days, spend time with the managers of the restaurants, spend time with the board, listen to their issues, explain our strategy again and again and get them to understand the Compass Group perspective . . . there is constant travel.

Francis Mackay, Chairman, Compass Group

Give others credit

When the company had around 1000 employees I realized that it was really me who slowed the growth of the company. I realized it was time to hire men and women who were smarter than me or who were at least complementary to what I was.

Pierre Bellon, Chairman, Sodexho Alliance

The leaders all disavow the claim that their leadership has been a key ingredient in their companies' successes. They claim they had luck, great people around them and more than a fair measure of good fortune. They are unassuming, and their diffidence turns out to be one of their enduring, and shared, traits. They take the blame for failures and give others the credit for their success. Although they seem to know all functional management disciplines well, they profess not to be the best at everything, and genuinely believe that without their great teams of people they were 'lucky to find', they would never be where they are today. They know where they need help and are not afraid to bring in the people they need, if they're smarter and faster. Imagine their approach as a coming together of the ability to teach and learn from a wide variety of people, and the willingness to support the subtle transformations wrought by dedicated employees throughout the organization is actually better suited to the everyday challenges of running a services business.

Francis Mackay is a fine example of ego-free leadership. He wants you to believe (as he does) that he has not been the master of his own success. He denies himself the pleasure of taking credit. Even when financial analysts and industry experts give Mackay credit, praise makes him uncomfortable. 'To actually go ahead and do what we have done, to drive and say, "We are going to take a risk, we are going to buy Accor's business for 600 million, nearly twice our size because the strategy is right." Didn't we think of the risks? I'm sure we did, but looking back, it looks like a huge amount of courage.' Silence takes over again, he smiles to himself. 'I think it was ignorance, probably ignorance at the time.' Mackay looks uncomfortable when the conversation turns to the subject of Francis Mackay. His face tightens. 'Probably 80% of the business has been *good luck*. Whenever I say that, people think "He is a very modest chap", but it is the truth. None of our opportunities could have arisen and we could have been sitting here with the same vision but a complete lack of success.'

True entrepreneurs

J. Philip-Sørensen and Lars Nørby Johansen:
Brash decisions and a sharp eye for opportunity

Group 4 Falck is largely what it is today because of Sørensen's ability to make snap decisions and explore new territory and because of Nørby's ability to pull Falck out of its public services corner and create a new Group 4 Falck service business.

Sørensen is not a man to hesitate. Once he decides, he fully supports and encourages an idea, a project or a person. Usually he's right. How else could he have built a thriving global organization? It is this instinct that has persuaded him to move into some new areas, such as prison and court services work, where some of his competitors have feared to tread. As he whisks around the Group's operating companies, visiting offices with his black boxes and talking to managers, he seems to have an uncanny ability to spot problems, notice current or imminent challenges or future opportunities before others.

Linda Sharpe suggests that the key to Group 4's successful organic growth was Sørensen's ability – entrepreneurial, strong, direct – to sense pioneering opportunity where others did not see it, such as in Poland, Hungary, the Czech Republic, Russia, India and Kazakhstan. According to Sharpe, Sorensen and his managers 'lead from the front', by doing what they believe and being very open about it.

> *One very good example was when we (the Group) moved into Poland and decided to set up a joint venture there. A public company, with its shareholders, would never have done it. But Sørensen believed passionately that Poland would be a country of the future and he was absolutely right.*
> Linda Sharpe, Principal, Group 4 Falck Academy

From 1988 when Lars Nørby Johansen became CEO of Falck, he set out to grow the company, yet, according to Nels Petersen, Director Group Communications, Group 4 Falck, he always followed a 'two-track social commitment': running and continuously developing good, healthy business on a sound commercial basis while also retaining the business concept on which Sophus Falck had built the company back in 1906: aiding people in need and preventing, or at least limiting, accidents. Throughout, Nørby Johansen has, as Petersen puts it, 'shown a remarkable ability to predict and evaluate general trends in society, both in domestic and international matters'. He has cultivated a strong domestic and international network, so he's always informed about what transpires in politics, national and international finance, industry and culture. He has the ability, for example, after a two-day in-house seminar, to sum up 'precisely the issues that need more work'. And he has come up with ideas for a number of successful Falck products, among them psychological crisis therapy for individuals, businesses and public authority subscribers.

Francis Mackay: A man for all detail

Francis Mackay is famous for his hands-on interest in detail – an entrepreneurial bent. When Mackay met Waldemar Schmidt at the World Economic Forum 2002 in New York, for example, a gala evening at the New York Stock Exchange was put on for the guests. As Schmidt and Mackay wandered from floor to floor, they passed a kitchen. Mackay immediately went in to find out, one, if it was a Compass business (it was not), and what was going on with the staff. Those who work with Mackay know this curiosity to see what's going on anywhere in the food services business. Swing your lens away from Mackay and onto the wider Compass Group and you see what an ex-marketeer of the Group calls Compass Group's major reason for success: its decentralized, entrepreneurial culture with a minimum of bureaucracy.

Pierre Bellon: Allowing two mistakes

Sodexho's unique brand is a kind of 'entrepreneurship with limits'. Pierre Bellon expects – demands, some would argue – of his managers that they think and act like entrepreneurs. If you're a site manager, and you have an idea, try it out. Innovate. Just make sure it harmonizes with company values. For an innovation to win an award at the Sodexho Innovation

Forum it has to have been up and running for six months. This rule ensures that people don't wait for some higher powers to give their blessing. It also requires a wide tolerance for mistakes. Everyone at Sodexho knows the innovation rule: *You have the right to make two mistakes – more than two gets to be too much.* Listen to Michel Dubois:

> *What is fantastic, with Pierre Bellon's management, is that he has a strategic mind, he is an entrepreneur and he makes sure his managers are entrepreneurs. He always says, 'My best skill is to find and develop entrepreneurs.' Bellon gives an objective to people and then they are totally free, but because the company continuously trains them and communicates the strategic direction to them, they have no way not to be with the philosophy of the company because it is written on a plastic card, and in everybody's pocket . . . including those of more than 314 000 front-line employees.*
>
> Michel Dubois, retired Senior Vice President Strategy,
> Innovation and Quality, Sodexho Alliance

Dubois told us a great story of entrepreneurship when he remembered how Bellon, who thought that, with Glasnost, it was time for Sodexho to start working in Russia, gave him the company's first assignment in Russia. Using his Russian contacts Dubois got his feet in the door of a few large industry restaurants, and saw the terrible state their kitchens were in: 'Things were leaking, they never shut the ovens off because if they did, they would never be able to fire them up again. So, imagine, they were never cleaned!' Here was a chance to organize at least a minimally functional kitchen: Dubois decided to sell kitchen equipment (not exactly Sodexho's core business!) to these restaurants for a commission. He quickly signed deals with a handful of French manufacturers: equipment for ready cash, and Sodexho took a nice margin. Within a year his impromptu kitchen equipment sales were turning a profit. Since then, Dubois has been in touch with the Ministry of Interior Affairs and to the delight of the public servants, ended up restructuring their kitchen and preparing their meals. From the Ministry's kitchen, Sodexho started delivering food to Western businesses in Moscow and set up camp management activities on their remote sites. Thus began Sodexho's Russian food services business.

Make yourself obsolete

Now we have around 800 top managers of all nationalities who are people who have grown with Sodexho, who have the spirit of service and teamwork and progress. I am assured I can disappear without any problem.

Pierre Bellon, Chairman, Sodexho Alliance

Pierre Bellon's name appears on the membership lists of many professional organizations, such as MEDEF, a French business confederation dedicated to improving business in general. He created an organization called The Association for Progress in Management, which now has more than 3000 member entrepreneurs in 160 clubs in France. At some stage, he recalls, while he was shuttling around trying to better French society, Sodexho ran perfectly well without him. 'Everything went smoothly because I stayed out of the hair of my employees and because we have people with an entrepreneurial spirit.' Bellon, with the founder's blood pumping through his veins, was naturally concerned with succession, one of the toughest hurdles for any family business in the second or third generation, but his quest to 'make himself obsolete' has led to the best possible result: a company that can succeed without him, in the spirit of service, teamwork and progress.

J. Philip-Sørensen, like Bellon, has made himself obsolete as well. By 2000, he was ready to take a step back. He has become chairman of the non-executive board and now has a minority stake in the combined Group 4 Falck. Did his new, more distant role come easy?

First of all, I had to find out what the chairman of a public company does! That wasn't so difficult, but it was more difficult to find out what he doesn't do. I've had some hard lessons there and it has been a little bit difficult in the beginning to see the position of leader completely separately from myself. It has been difficult for me and I think anyone coming from a family company in the way I give the transition some serious thought because some people won't be able to make that change. I hope I have made it. I've tried my best and I still enjoy it, and I think that's the most important thing.

J. Philip-Sørensen, Chairman of the Board of Directors, Group 4 Falck

Group 4 Falck has a confidential succession plan the managers know nothing about, but as Richard Sutton, Group 4 Falck Human Resources

Director, points out, 'It is important to have a succession plan in place, to be prepared.' The everyday part of this succession process is pushing the level of authority down to the operating countries, not only because every country is different, but also to prepare them for a change of leadership.

Intimate business knowledge

In order to grow their companies to the size they have and change the industry to what it is now, the CEOs must be multi-skilled. They are, as we've seen, inspiring leaders of people, but they are also M&A experts, HR experts who work with union leaders and works councils and play a strong hand in selecting and developing their top managers. If needed, they act as sales people, with personal contact with local staff and customers, and at times they have more than the usual contacts with analysts and shareholders. They appear to take part in a wider variety of management activities than the average chairman or CEO. As role models, they can get involved in even the smallest details. The deep understanding of the business in the case of Sørensen and Bellon goes back to the days when their businesses were so small that they were involved in every detail themselves. Recall Sørensen's claim that he straightens the picture in the office of a remote site – anything to improve service.

Long history with the company

During the long stretches that Bellon, Berglund, Mackay, Nørby and Sørensen have been leading their companies, the average company would have had several CEOs. The five are 'long-timers' but they are not the only ones. They built around themselves a management group of equally committed 'long-timers'. Many senior managers in these companies have 'worked their way up' the rungs of the organization. This has resulted in strong company cultures based on values and principles (like initiative and responsibility) that the four companies established 20 or 30 years ago and are still pushing. Owing to often very long careers with the company, senior managers also have a very good understanding of the details in the industry, which helps them maintain a trust-based interaction with front-line employees.

At Securitas, the original management team (excluding the representatives of acquired companies), have been at the company on average more than 12 years each. Since Thomas Berglund has been at the wheel, only one senior executive – who came from outside Securitas – has left the team.

At Sodexho, all but one key person joined during the first 20 years of the company, and all were intimately involved in defining the business model. On average the senior executives have been working for Sodexho for more than 23 years.

Of the 16 directors, senior employees and advisors at Compass Group, four, including Mackay have been with the company more than 15 years, the rest have tenures averaging six years, with a handful of key players – Group Chief Executive, Group Finance Director and Deputy Chairman – for around a decade.

Questions for service leaders

1. Do you understand the evolution of your industry, and do you have a plan for your company's place in it?

2. Do you see ways to shape your industry to your and your customers' advantage?

3. Are your vision, mission and values simple and clear? How could you further simplify or clarify them? How do you ensure that they are understood throughout your company? How could you promote better understanding?

4. Do you spend enough time away from the office meeting staff, customers and other stakeholders? What could you do to spend more time meeting these key groups?

5. What in your behaviour in the organization do you really want to transfer into the organization? What can you do to increase the strength of this role-modelling?

6. Do you have a succession plan?

7. What entrepreneurial initiatives have people in your company recently taken? How have you rewarded them?

5

Passion for people

The key to our success at Group 4 Falck is the way we handle people. You get to work with IT and all sorts of electronic gadgets, but basically and fundamentally it comes down to the questions: How do you manage your people? Do they believe you? Do they trust you? You cannot escape that. We're not selling sausages, we're selling services produced by people! Point number one is recruiting the right people. Point number two is training them. And point number three is keeping them.

J. Philip-Sørensen, Chairman of the Board of Directors, Group 4 Falck

All leaders care, to some extent, for their companies, but not all leaders truly care for their people. The five leaders in this book do. Their precept is: Every individual counts. Their companies follow suit.

Ninety percent of the role of the chief executive or even chairman is getting your key people to be in the right frame of mind: well-trained, well-motivated, well-rewarded. The chairman's role is more about asking, 'Where is the company going?' and 'Where are the people coming from?' Fundamentally, what you are about is convincing people to be successful. So if we are working together, my whole reason for being here is to make you successful. So the only reason I am suggesting this particular direction or strategy or this operational issue is to make you successful . . . in terms of reward, status and image.

Francis Mackay, Executive Chairman, Compass

Compass Group, Group 4 Falck, Securitas and Sodexho, says an industry expert, 'treat their people very, very well'. Sørensen demonstrates: on the way to the interview room, he tells us he thanked the Lausanne taxi driver for the excellent ride from the airport to IMD. 'You know why?', he asks, 'because the drive was indeed fine, but, more importantly, the next time the driver picks someone up, he will feel good about providing an excellent service, and that's what we need!' In all four companies we have seen a deep respect for people of all levels and a grand belief in their potential.

> *If there are any secrets, it is the simple secret that you have to love people if you are going to be in the people business, you have to make them stronger and independent, not make them dependent on you.*
>
> Thomas Berglund, CEO, Securitas

Every time we asked anybody who professed to know anything about the service industry we heard the same refrain: it all comes down to people. More than any other industry, the service industry depends on motivated, committed, loyal, well-trained staff. Service winners understand what drives people and seek to motivate in cost-efficient ways.

> *In our business, our services are delivered by people, not by machines. We're not selling products, we're not selling technology, we're selling services. And those services are delivered by people. And if those people are not happy or satisfied in their work, they can't deliver the services that our customers demand. It is that simple. So unless you have this caring for people, you can't deliver quality services to your customers because our 'products' are people.*
>
> Lars Nørby Johansen, CEO, Group 4 Falck

In food and security services, you have a limited margin potential. The key to keeping your contracts is employing people who live up to the conditions negotiated with the client. These people have to be motivated. Since the wages are not at the high end of the wage scale, the four companies have to find other ways to motivate staff and get the job done. All four companies do this by offering shares, incentive schemes and internal promotion. Research shows that, in those countries where people are given a decent wage and effective training, turnover is lower and quality is better – everybody wins. The customer most of all. This makes a lot of business sense. Why? The answer is simple: For any service company, the most significant risk factors for growth, financial position and operational results are people.

In service you have no – or hardly any – tangible product. Quality and customer satisfaction depend on how well your people serve your clients. Succeeding in security, for example, is also about building and keeping an impeccable image and reputation. Tarnish a service company's reputation, and it may take years to shine it. Since security and food service are labour-intensive, failing to hire sufficient personnel in certain markets harms business. Imagine Group 4 Falck's challenge of finding qualified people in a remote area such as Kazakhstan. People can make – or break – its reputation – and its business.

A security employee told us that, for years, security guards were required to sign off when they made one of many regularly-repeated site visits. All too often, they visited once, but signed many times. With guards who perform their duties like this, your reputation will be sorely hurt, and you probably won't achieve greatness. Even if you have a great and stirring vision, a 10-year week-by-week business plan, the world's most sensitive infra-red digital surveillance system will get you nowhere if you've got mediocre, unmotivated, uninterested people giving mediocre results. If the people you have working for you hopped on board merely to earn a living, without special pride in your services, you cannot respond to your challenges. You can't afford to have sloppy, uncaring people carrying the flag. Yet, with the right people on board, you can adapt to an ever-changing world of service needs and keep offering reliable, trustworthy services.

They must have this sense of 'I want a job with some responsibility. I want to be solely identified with that responsibility. I don't want to be a member of a chain.' Those are the people we are looking for – men and women. They don't have to be big and strong, that's not an issue, they have to have the right mental attitude – they must want to provide a service and enjoy it.
    J. Philip-Sørensen, Chairman of the Board of Directors, Group 4 Falck

Service employees are a comparatively weighty financial factor in and of themselves. Security companies spend around 80% of their costs on personnel; food services 40%. In contrast, labour costs in manufacturing companies are often only 20% or less. Any increase in labour costs – wages, turnover, insurance, pensions, social security and other employee benefits like training – has an enormous impact on the company's profitability. But their ability to pass on even small price increases is limited by contract and by market acceptance.

Furthermore, to generate organic growth and to integrate acquired companies, our four companies depend on employee know-how and expertise. They depend, to some extent, on *key* employees to retain and pass-on this know-how. The problem is, even when you find ways to train and motivate your employees, turnover in services is very high.

Global data on labour turnover in the service industry are difficult to mine, probably because most service companies are very decentralized and keep the records – if they keep them at all – at local sites only. One safe conclusion: turnover in the service industry is a high hurdle for our companies. Another safe conclusion: if your turnover increases, expect a jump in costs, a drop in quality and a drop in customer retention rates. Consider an example from Group 4 Falck in Great Britain: in 1998, employee turnover at Group 4 Falck Total Security – UK exceeded 60%. The company put a quality process in place. Attention to the quality systems improved both customer and employee satisfaction rates. Turnover sank to below 30%. Customer satisfaction improved further, and so too did the financials.

By offering people good wages, strong incentives, chances to move up and grow professionally, the four companies keep employee turnover relatively low. And low employee turnover means having a critical mass of employees who have had long tenures and therefore understand, appreciate and stand for the companies' values. Whatever they are.

The four service companies have deep roots in the European tradition of respecting employees. Perhaps more so than companies in other continents. In Northern European countries, laws underpin the importance of front-line staff: any company larger than 50 employees has to have at least one member of staff on its board. Scandinavian statutes require these firms to have one employee representative for every two board members the shareholders elect. On the Securitas board sit a service technician, a response guard and chief safety representative, a staff engineer and a team leader. Group 4 Falck has two rescue officers, an information officer and an executive secretary.

Again Nørby Johansen: Effective management means more than organizing people and defining their jobs, an attitude he reduces to 'seeing [people] as factors of production'. Managing well means 'feeling for your people, wanting to develop them', not only giving them good salaries, but also 'giving them life opportunities, and empowering them'. That tradition has grown most strongly in Europe, where it was bolstered by a simple insight: *people are the most important resource in a service company*. As Nørby Johansen believes, the reason that the tradition of caring for your people came out of Europe, especially the Nordic countries, has to do with the size of the public sector there, the tradition of more and more interplay between public and the private sector – 'a long-term tradition for strong trade unions in a unified trade-union movement with very strong actors that force you to listen to their advice and their desires and wants, otherwise you can't get on with your business'. In this tradition, individuals make the difference – getting the right ones, and keeping them, is a most important aspect of running a service business.

Compass Group, Group 4 Falck, Securitas and Sodexho care. Care runs through their cultures, their policies and their systems. It runs through the ways they *recruit, integrate and develop*, and *retain* people. They focus extensively on HR processes. They grow and develop their people. They instil pride; create confidence; build teams; provide resources. They delegate responsibility far out into the distant reaches of the organization, close to customers in day-to-day work. They offer employees a fair wage, decent jobs and good working conditions. They take a long-term view of recruiting, and adhere closely to careful recruiting procedures. They pay a lot – in time and money – for training. To keep top performers, they promote from within, map out clear internal career paths and offer broad incentive programmes. All four companies *work closely with unions*, like partners, not adversaries. They know that only by working *with* these politically powerful groups can they improve the conditions in the industry and ensure the dedication of their employees.

SODEXHO HUMAN RESOURCES POLICY

- Emphasize promotion from within

- Attach particular importance to hiring young people

- Promote the hiring of local people at all our host countries

- Recognize the importance of interpersonal skills

- Encourage empowerment and self-management

Recruit

Even if our companies have managed to reduce their rate of staff turnover well below the industry average, the number of leavers and new recruits is staggering. Thirty percent turnover on a global scale still means 60 000 to 100 000 leavers and new recruits per year per company. This is why Compass Group, Group 4 Falck, Securitas and Sodexho pay a lot of attention to recruitment.

The four companies practise their own brand of wisdom, pretty much summed up by: *when it comes to offering the best services day in, day out, you have to begin with 'who'* – front-line security officer, waitress, cook, teller. But how do our four companies find such people in a low-wage, low-skill environment? What kind of people are the four companies looking for?

Sodexho: Hire and develop entrepreneurs

Patrice Douce, retired Sodexho COO, believes that 'one of the key success factors of Sodexho is the ability to hire people with a potential that's higher than needed'. This has meant that, as the company was growing fast, sometimes as much as 25% a year, with a doubling every three years (in some countries company growth was 100% in less than a year), it was never caught off guard either by a shortage of good people or by people who weren't of the right calibre.

Bernard Carton, retired CFO of Sodexho, echoes Douce's claim that Sodexho emphasizes attitude: 'We prefer to hire people based on people skills and an insight into our business rather than on functional skills alone. We shift people around anyway: from operations to finance, vice versa or in between any other functions.' When the company was looking for Carton's successor, it narrowed the choice to several internal candidates who were 'all selected based on their level of integration into the company and the respect they had earned from their colleagues as a manager, rather than as a specialist'.

Ever since I started at Sodexho three years ago as a chef in a smaller restaurant I too wanted to become a Unit Manager. Sodexho offered me structured training right from the start, along with job opportunities in relation to my improving qualifications. I developed skills I didn't even know I had, because my superiors always had great trust in me and supported my career. My job is versatile and demanding and that makes it very rewarding at the same time.

Sascha Rath, Unit Manager, Allianz Berlin, Germany, Sodexho Alliance

(source: Sodexho website)

Compass Group: Professional development, decent hours and career options the world over

We have made the food service a business that people want to join . . . most of our businesses work from 8 to 5, whereas if you are going to work in a restaurant, you are working from 8 to 2 in the morning.

Francis Mackay, Chairman, Compass Group

Compass Group has become a widely respected name in the food service business because of its favourable personnel policies. Food service workers know and widely respect Compass Group:

I would not even want to work for the best five-star hotel in town, because they are so local in their view and I would have many fewer development opportunities. I love this profession and I have always wanted to progress in restaurant management. Eurest (a Compass Group brand) gives me this opportunity. We have regular training but we can also try out new approaches ourselves, for special occasions, for example. I have always liked to travel, and I hope that one day I can go to another site in the international Eurest organization.

Eurest restaurant supervisor, Compass Group

This enviable position allows the company to recruit, even from the hoity-toity world of fine dining. A regional manager for Eurest noted that the company recently snared a prominent chef from one of Sir Terence Conran's upscale restaurants.[1] Top-quality people don't merely have to be highly skilled for Compass Group to be interested, they need to be sharp. This desire for smarts begins at the top. Francis Mackay, for example, looks for people who are smarter than he is. But he expects more:

It's about employing people that you enjoy working with, intelligent people who are committed to the Group, and with whom you will enjoy setting direction.

Francis Mackay, Chairman, Compass Group

---

[1] Sir Terence Conran is the founder of Habitat and owner of some very trendy restaurants.

Securitas: Middle-class people with a fist in their pocket

In Berglund's words, Securitas people need to be 'a little more interested in the job than the average'. Securitas wants 'middle-class men or women with "a fist in their pockets", [people] who want to show they can do better. Not someone born with a golden spoon [in his/her mouth]'. Many Securitas people come from that background and have, for varying reasons, a special drive to succeed. A good example, from Berglund, is Juan Vallejo, currently Securitas' divisional president security systems Europe:

> He was six years old when he came to Sweden with his Spanish parents. They were immigrants, from fairly poor circumstances. Forty years ago it wasn't easy being an immigrant in Sweden. Being a poor Spanish guy in Swedish society gave him a special drive.
>
> Thomas Berglund, CEO, Securitas

Securitas' screening criteria for guards and other positions make a high bar for job applicants. For example, the company's Swedish branch wants future guards to have a high school graduation diploma, proof of a clean criminal record, fluency in Swedish and English, a minimum of 20 years old, good health, stamina and a balanced state of mental health.

Group 4 Falck: Not gears in wheels
but independent people who take responsibility

> Despite what people say, despite the fact that we are living in a society where the government looks after everything for us and we become slaves of the system, so to speak, there are still people in this world who like to be given responsibility. And those are the people we want to get hold of.
>
> J. Philip-Sørensen, Chairman of the Board of Directors, Group 4 Falck

Sørensen explains that people in Group 4 Falck must be independent, 'a bit of the entrepreneur themselves'. The company does have some degree of financial control, but, Sørensen adds, 'they must feel they run their own business'. This means the company gives them responsibility, a 'fair reward for what they do' and a chance to feel part of a team, a 'bigger team, like one of the Group companies or even the Group as a whole. [. . .] There is nothing so strong as a sense of belonging but still having your individualism respected and your individual duties to perform. [. . .] When those two meet you get a very strong management team.'

At Group 4 Falck, recruiting is a local matter. 'The only recruiting we do on a corporate level', says Richard Sutton, HR Director for the Group, 'is the recruitment of senior managers and expatriates. We are also available to help local markets with recruiting, for example if they need psychological testing done.' Locally, says Linda Sharpe, Principal, Group 4 Falck Academy, the company has 'quite specific methods for recruiting'. It 'profiles jobs to identify the real characteristics that make people in those management jobs do successfully. We know what an effective managing director looks like, what a successful finance or operations person looks like, give or take some cultural differences.'

Group 4 Falck HR people also analyse the characteristics in the people who leave after a short time. For external recruiting, it has 'quite a stringent assessment process like ability tests in the native language of the candidate in numerical reasoning and verbal reasoning. We don't look for the highest scores but candidates must reach our minimum standards.' The company adapts its standards to each locality. 'We benchmark with senior management graduate levels across the world in each individual country.'

GETTING THE RIGHT PEOPLE: GROUP 4 FALCK RECRUITING PROCESS FOR SITE MANAGERS

1. Personnel specification

2. Recruiting officer interviews

3. Five-day initial training course

4. Specific site training

5. Appraisal training

6. Development

What is Group 4 Falck looking for in its managers? 'Not geniuses!', says Sharpe, 'We profile the personality, we don't take people who are negative, non-people focused, not team players. We give a high weighting to people management skills.' The company turns down 'quite a lot of people' who don't 'suit the culture'. Sørensen follows the rule that a supervisor should not supervise more people than he knows the names of – and preferably the names of the family too. Again Sharpe:

> We are good at mobilizing large numbers of middle management semi-professionals. In the UK prisons business, for example, we have hired our prison directors from outside, but underneath that we developed our own teams by recruiting people who have good interpersonal and communication skills and then we have trained them in technical skills. If we need a specialist, we hire one, but we try to grow the team inside.
>
> Linda Sharpe, Principal, Group 4 Falck Academy

As for rescuers in the safety sector of Group 4 Falck, HR usually has no need to advertise. According to Johnny Eikeland, Group 4 Falck has a waiting list in Denmark alone of 500–1000 people who want to join.

> We don't have to advertise. It's a high-profile job. [As part of the recruiting process], potential rescuers take an examination and a psychological test, and then they have an interview with a human resources person to find out how they might perform.
>
> Johnny Eikeland, Employee Representative on the Board, Group 4 Falck

Attitude is indeed one of the most important selection criteria says Nels Petersen, Group Communications Director of Group 4 Falck, but ultimately the company's recruiting differs from country to country. In some countries it is normal for security people to come from the army, and they may come with the wrong attitude, thinking that Group 4 Falck is a private army. After all, in some countries, Group 4 Falck people do carry weapons. From an army background or not, Sørensen and Nørby Johansen want independent spirits who are willing to start at the bottom and work up.

> I have a rule that no one should become a supervisor, let alone a manager, unless he/she has been out working as a security guard, both on permanent assignment and out on patrol. There's nothing like working all night and coming home in the morning and feeling dead beat and trying to sleep while you have screaming kids in

the house. You have to learn to cope with that. I tell anyone who wants to work as a security guard: 'Buy a black blind for your bedroom window.' I know what it's like because I have been a guard myself.

J. Philip-Sørensen, Chairman of the Board of Directors, Group 4 Falck

Integrate and develop

Succeeding at service goes way beyond screening and recruiting great employees. The right people may be motivated, open to change, flexible, ambitious and reliable, but they need to be able to integrate themselves (or to 'be integrated') into the 'team', and become part of a strong corporate culture. One important service company tool for integration is developing people's knowledge and skills. Perhaps this is why, as our four companies have been shaping their industries over the last 10 to 20 years, they have made it a pillar of their management philosophy to care for and develop their employees. Besides pumping a thick and steady stream of money and resources into their development programmes (about 2% of sales for Group 4 Falck and Securitas), managers in all four service winners also spend significant amounts of time participating in and leading different training modules.

The four companies arrange training in all countries of operation, often offering programmes that stretch well beyond the required letter of the 'training' law. As each company refines its services, becoming either more specialized or more multiservice, requirements become clearer, and the company responds by preparing its people in special programmes – in Sodexho, for example, on ageing or diet requirements; in Securitas, on linking IT and security; in Group 4 Falck, on emergency medical assistance; or even the most common topics that fill the brochures of executive MBA programmes. Always the theory is linked to the daily reality of the employee on the front line: top executive training, lower-, middle- and upper-level management training, group leader training, shift leader training, the whole seemingly endless array of leadership training for all levels, with in-depth study of the company model and long discussions of its values. In the training programmes of our four firms, all have their place, in varying degrees and forms.

But the most important training at these four companies happens at work. Managers coach their co-workers, and they follow up. Succeeding, even 'just working', in service means constantly developing – with employees, customers, shareholders and external organizations. The learning never stops. The leader, from the head of a group of guards in Berlin to the head chef of a small bank-catering operation in New York, is a committed teacher, mentor, coach, master of dialogue and role model. That's because, in these companies, people really do make a difference.

Group 4 Falck: Developing people, even in the remotest places

The right people don't need to understand the business in detail, but they do need to have the right attitude. We don't want them to come with all sorts of fancy ideas like being part of a private army or thinking they've got authority because they have a uniform on with a lot of glossy things on it. Once they're in, they must learn the details of the business. We teach them how. We give them all the knowledge they require. We teach them the Group 4 Falck method.

    J. Philip-Sørensen, Chairman of the Board of Directors, Group 4 Falck

According to Sørensen, Group 4 Falck spends more money on recruiting and training than on selling its services (recall that up to 2% of turnover goes into training). Sales, marketing, PR and advertising budgets are far below that. To get a feeling for how hard Group 4 Falck works to train and develop its people, consider the French branch of the company, the subsidiary called Euroguard. Euroguard employees get their guarding curriculum – every minute and every piece of it – at the company's own guard school, L'Institute Francais de Formation et d'Ingénieur Securitaire (IFFS, or, in English, The French Institute for the Education of Security Guards). The company has three levels of education: Level 1: fire fighting, safety, legislation; Level 2: regulation, crisis management; Level 3: security management. As guards advance up the organization, they follow the curriculum that corresponds both to the company's expectations for them and their new responsibilities at their new, higher ('after advancement') level.

Group 4 Falck Academy
Developing Management Potential Programme

BUSINESS ACUMEN MODULE

- The scope of strategic management
- Understanding and practising the marketing mix
- Understanding and using key measures of business performance
- Understanding and interpreting key economic indicators
- Understanding the difference between cash and profit
- The key elements of, and practise in, commercial negotiation
- Developing and applying a business plan
- Alternative models for raising profitability
- Managing the trade-offs between short-term profits and long-term sustainable business performance

According to Richard Sutton, Group Human Resources Director, the managers of acquired units and new managers go through an international induction programme. Beyond the usual introductory courses in history, they take *Communication and Visual Standards, Understanding Shareholder Management, Key Elements in Guarding Operations: Customers, Employees, and Service Delivery* and they make a visit to a local company. They learn about Group 4 Falck's culture and values, but they also 'see the world beyond the country border and meet peers from around the world who have the same issues as they do, so they build a network to learn from each other even after the programme'.

In its quality process, launched in 1988, Group 4 formalized its staff training. Four days of first line introductory training in Group 4 Total Security, for example, takes place during the first four days of employment. This training incorporates and exceeds the training standard set down by the United Kingdom Security Industry Training Organization (an average security firm in the UK trains its new employees for a maximum of two days). Richard Sutton describes the training in this way:

It pays a lot of attention to professional issues, such as how guards should behave, dress, react. We also emphasize values: the managers of an acquired company may learn, to their surprise, that they are not allowed to give even the smallest bribe to any official, even if in their country this is common practice for getting contracts signed. The manager also learns about the four main Group 4 Falck 'value drivers': create high organic growth focusing on areas with above-average margins, increase earnings and operating margins whilst retaining competitive prices, reduce net operating assets to reduce net capital ties up, and growth through an active acquisition policy. We work hard on instilling Group 4 Falck ethics into newly acquired staff because they carry the responsibility for the image of the whole Group.

Richard Sutton, Group HR Director, Group 4 Falck

Each employee returns to the classroom after three months (the end of the probationary period) for further training. In the year 2000, two thousand new starters went through the programme, at a total training spend of around €1.6 million. Employees in France who work with customers who have special requirements attend the IFFS for special educational content. For those who work in high risk areas – such as petro-chemical plants – there are courses on first aid, CPR and other first-aid medical treatments. Courses on handling mechanical devices such as air conditioners, elevators and heating pumps are available for guards who work in heavy industry or large office complexes. Since Group 4 Falck has guards who work with international transport, the IFFS offers language classes to help its people get up to speed in the necessary two to three languages.

The net result of all these training programmes for employees is that, as Johnny Eikeland says,

I am in education all the time – it started with the firefighting academy, ambulance school, rescue school, the courses on animal rescue, courses on how car engines work and how to get the car started. That's the case for everybody . . . when I went into management they were always telling me, 'we want you to go to this course because we think it will be good for you in the future', for example, communication.

Johnny Eikeland, Employee Representative on the Board, Group 4 Falck

Group 4 Falck in Kazakhstan shows the company's commitment to training in practice. Kazzinc (part of the Swiss-based Glencore group, the second largest private company in the world, with a turnover in the region of US$40 billion), one of Kazakhstan's largest mining projects, with mines in three Northern Kazak cities, decided to employ Group 4 Falck to look after some serious security needs at its Leninagorsk site. Group 4 Falck Kazakhstan has also been contracted to guard a power station, again working with an international client, AES from the United States. These two contract successes follow continuous growth since 1997 for Group 4 Falck Kazakhstan, which now has 1400 employees. The company believes it would never have won these contracts, nor experienced steady growth, if it had not invested heavily in what it calls 'international levels of training' for its mostly local recruits and then demanded integrity and quality from them. Most of the staff, in this case formerly military staff and security personnel, receive not only the basic training required by local laws, but also get specialist schooling from Group 4 Falck Security Support Service trainers as well as the local companies' training staff. This degree and richness of training, the company believes, sets its security staff a cut above the competition in the region. One of the major client's managers says, now that he's seen Group 4 Falck at work, he can finally 'sleep at night'.

Compass Group: Decentralized training initiatives

Compass Group has not started a food services school, and it hasn't got its own central training facility. Neither would make much sense, considering the company's business model. But it has found the equivalent in a number of its segments: one example is the Eurest Dining Academy, which ran its first classes in May 1996 in Elmhurst, Illinois (USA) under the banner: Reshaping Our Region. The one-day seminar, a series of 75-minute classes framed by keynote speeches by the then Eurest Dining Services President, was open to all Eurest employees. No matter what their interest – finance, purchasing, cooking, marketing or legal issues – Eurest employees from the Chicago region found something professionally relevant or interesting. There was *Accounting 101*, the basics of daily and weekly Eurest food service operations, for new unit managers, chefs and assistant managers heading up to management positions. *Practical Purchasing for the '90s* gave an overview of bid practices with Eurest's preferred/required product list. The *Magic of the Eye* and *Crystal Images* focused on ice carving. *Sell Smart Merchandising* covered basic marketing. For the food-minded there were *Basta Past*, *Woks of Fun, Branding and Beyond* and *Healthy Bodies, Hungry Minds*. Other topics included the Family Medical Leave Act, client relations and account retention and ways to measure customer satisfaction. Of course, each contract company under the Compass Group umbrella runs training as it sees fit, but Compass Group expects it to 'see fit' and makes sure all the employees in the Group are getting the training they need.

To create a challenging environment and develop managers inside the wide walls of the company, Compass Group has its own brand of extensive internal training. For example, it encourages employees to move around and gain experience in different types of restaurants, which has the nice side-effect of strengthening corporate values and improving employees' knowledge of the ins and outs of the business.

> *When we first entered the United States, the biggest issue was not wages – it was training. So we put in a very significant training programme, and this improved employee satisfaction enormously.*
> Francis Mackay, Chairman, Compass Group

Like the three other service leaders, Compass Group prefers to select on people skills rather than technical skills and then invest heavily in bringing the skills of the new recruits up to speed. The company recently hired a new CEO for its French business. The man in question had been the vice president of Hertz Europe, and he had also managed the Forte Hotel business. He came with all the right people skills, but, as Francis Mackay notes, 'we had to take account of the fact that his knowledge of the contract catering business was limited, and therefore his induction programme had to be different from other people's'. This willingness to tailor training to individual managers is the norm at Compass Group.

Compass Group's management development programme gives people – 30–80 at a time, depending on the programme – the chance to share knowledge and to experience that they have all got similar issues to address. To Francis Mackay this is the most valuable output of the management development programme: to get people to work together across borders.

Beyond training programmes, Compass Group shares best practice through its line organizations. Mackay admits to not sharing best practices as well as he'd like to, but the company has, nevertheless, 'developed an intranet system "Mercury", a source of information, names and addresses. If you're talking to a large technology company, you can go into the catalogue and find somebody who knows about that company. If you're talking to IBM, then you will talk to so and so, who is based in the States, because he has more business with IBM than anybody else.'

Securitas: Raising the training standard in security

Fifteen years ago, a guard had two days of training here before he went on active duty. Today it takes up to three months before we can let a guard work on his or her own.

Roger Karlsson, Group Leader of Securitas' Pharmacia AB's
site in Uppsala, Sweden

In Sweden – Securitas' role model market for training – new hires go through at least six weeks of initial basic training, much of it at the company guarding school, Väktarskolan, in Sweden, and then follow additional, customized courses for special assignments, such as being receptionists, environmental guards or IT guards. In Sweden, the company requires 200 or more hours of yearly on-going training for a guard. In most other countries the number of training hours is lower, depending on local practices, but – also due to the pressure Securitas puts on raising the standards in the industry – training is gaining increasing priority in more and more countries.

For front-line people, Securitas offers, in addition to basic training, an extensive range of specialized training to meet customers' growing demands for specific services, for example training for receptionists and fire protection guards. Employees in airport security have a special Airport Security Training Centre in Brussels for guards and managers from around Europe. The demands on employees in airport security, especially after 11 September 2001, have risen even further. Not only do they have to be skilled in security, they also have to work closely with passengers in a multi-lingual and multinational environment with high demands on service. Other specialized development programmes serve operators at alarm monitoring stations, which feature high demands on perceptiveness, multi-tasking and language skills. Security personnel in the United States are getting more training than ever before, to meet new and increasing demands on guards of high-rise buildings, major events, oil refineries and nuclear power plants, including evacuation procedures and identifying suspicious packages. Some training happens at branch offices, and some at customers' facilities.

The Securitas Pharmacia site has 30 guards, of whom 40% are women, and all of whom walk an average of 25 kilometres per night shift. The site has 6000 alarms connected to the gatehouse and gets, on average, 700 cars and 150 visitors a day passing through the front gate. Recently, [Securitas Uppsala] added a clause to contracts that stipulates that each guard will get 10 hours a year to update his or her training so Securitas can continuously improve the quality of services.

> Securitas and Pharmacia are working together to make the guard's job more stimulating by eliminating boring and monotonous tasks . . . [because] we are not served well if the guards don't feel highly motivated.
>
> Bengt Ljung, Pharmacia AB

In addition to guard training, Securitas provides leadership training at various levels, nationally and internationally. The first step is group leader training, where managers learn what it means to be a leader and to follow up on one's operations. At the national level, leadership training is available to branch and area managers to help them better understand the Securitas model and their own businesses. In these sessions the Securitas Toolbox is used extensively.

Securitas has also set up so-called 'Competence Centres' to showcase best practices in the company. Employees visit centres for information, inspiration or training. Spain houses the centre for time-sharing security services for smaller customers. Sweden houses the centre for combined solutions for large customers.

Every two years, branch managers meet to go through the latest thinking in the company. The tools from the toolbox again play an important role in conveying the company message, since all senior managers use it to tailor their presentations. At the year 2000 meeting, 1000 branch managers met to exchange experiences; senior executives tried to make it as compelling as possible by not just using slides but by putting on a CNN-like news show, role playing and interviewing each other.

At the Group level, a management programme for 50 (2002) managers takes place each year, requiring them to meet five to six times, each time for three days, with project work in between. The meetings happen at different company sites, and Berglund runs that programme himself, which takes 20 days out of his yearly agenda. Upon completion of the year-long Securitas Executive Training (candidates must pass final exams!) participants receive the secret symbol that represents what it is like to be a Securitas manager:

We don't talk bullshit, we stand in it!

Securitas does not use consultants or management professors to facilitate and run training programmes. Explains Berglund, without the slightest note of superiority:

> *We have found that if the training is going to be really instrumental, it needs to be very precise and based on cases from our people's everyday lives. In my experience, very few people – CEOs included – have the ability to abstract from a general situation the ideas that will be instrumental in their daily working lives. It's a fairly difficult process, intellectually, to draw the right conclusion for yourself from someone else's situation. So we use Securitas people to lead the management development programme – anyone who has a good or a bad story that others can learn from.*
>
> Thomas Berglund, CEO, Securitas

The company's own managers serve as its consultants and troubleshooters. The six modules of the yearly training take place at six different company sites.

> *We go around and we meet in six different cities every year and we use the operation in that city as a base. In November 2001, the 25 managers met in Madrid. They 'penetrated' the operation, the alarm people into the alarm business, the guarding people into the guarding and the cash handling into the cash handling, acting as consultants.*
>
> Thomas Berglund, CEO, Securitas

By involving Group management, country managers and management groups in different countries, exciting meetings and discussions result. By

using its own business as a basis for training, with managers as teachers, and
. visits to other countries, the company 'increases mutual understanding and
gets closer to the new generation of leaders'.

Sodexho: The spirit of progress

Because Sodexho believes that training is the key to personal growth, it
expects its people to take part in its extensive training programmes, most of
which take place at the company's own management and training
institutes. The group gives its people, at all levels, on-the-job training
that it ties as closely as possible to field experience. The company provides
operational managers, senior executives and front-line staff with a wide
range of training programmes to help them improve their skills and
understanding of the business. In France, Italy and Sweden, operational
managers take part in training session in various areas, such as client
relations, cost management and motivating teams. Restaurant service staff
have training programmes on themes ranging from customer tastes and
eating patterns to food safety, to the care and sterilization of equipment.

> Our people are very important to me and I am very proud that so many of our
> employees have developed into general managers. Somehow Sodexho is like a
> machine that produces entrepreneurs.[2]
>
> Pierre Bellon, Chairman, Sodexho Alliance

The Sodexho Management Institute (SMI), an international and
multicultural place for meeting, exchanges and sharing, launched in
1992, aims to contribute to the permanent progress of the Group's Senior
Executives by helping them to become what the company calls
'Entrepreneurs the Group needs for guaranteeing its growth'. Above and
beyond specific management training, Sodexho executives learn and
progress by taking on new responsibilities, learning new functions,
collaborating with work groups and project teams, and by going through
training that focuses on experience, best practice sharing and group

---

[2] Translated from 'la voix des medias', transcript of a radio interview by Didier Ades on
17 December 2001.

discussions. Sodexho Management Institute bolsters this learning by serving as a conduit for the Group's values; it is, as the company calls it, 'a place of research, a platform for ideas and know-how' – a place for creating 'real networks'. The Institute is an important forum for sharing best practices at the corporate level – sharing best practice is a top Sodexho priority – and for developing ideas and providing executives with the tools they need to grow the business and advance their careers. Each year, on average, 300 managers participate in the SMI programme. Institute sessions help them better understand the company's core values and enable them to promote Sodexho values when they return to their sites. The SMI programme consists of a five-year learning cycle, offering a variety of learning tools that cover topics like company history, strategies and policies.

On a national level, employees regularly go to local training institutes such as the Belgian Sodexho Academy, which the company opened in 1997. Not only does the academy improve the staff's skills and teach basic management principles, it also helps to implement core values and strategic objectives at the local level, and grows team spirit through various team activities. Sodexho creates a lot of the new knowledge for its participants itself as it invests heavily in research and innovation.

In 1999, for example, The Sodexho Research Institute on the Quality of Life published a research study that profiled senior citizens, and identified precisely the needs and lifestyle preferences that determine their satisfaction with everyday life. What does this have to do with training? Easy. The findings underpin Sodexho's service portfolio and, along with other, supplementary reports, reflect its quest to understand and improve senior citizens' experiences in retirement homes. In the United Kingdom, Sodexho dieticians enhance food service in nursing and residential homes, with staff acting on ideas from a Sodexho-published nutrition guidebook to ensure that dishes are attractive and appetizing – and served hot! Sodexho training programmes help staff members better understand ageing issues, and show them how to develop better relationships with the elderly. Sodexho created a CD-ROM that trains catering and support staff; it showcases the Healthcare Worldwide Market Champion Group, giving examples from 18 countries of best practice in nutrition, multiservices solutions and human resources development.

Sodexho wants its development activities to help its people to 'take one step up the social ladder'. Around 85% of Sodexho's employees are operational staff, and of these, 80% are women. The training manager of the French Business and Industry subsidiary noticed that many of the women staff members were ill-at-ease around customers. According to the training manager, 'when a customer dropped a plate, the woman behind the counter was at a loss, and, to avoid dealing with the situation, would call the chef or site manager'. The training manager soon learned that his restaurant staff often felt intimidated by their customers in expensive suits.

He hired, at a special rate, a theatre for several two-day sessions. He invited make-up experts and hairdressers, and, in groups of 30, brought the front-line Sodexho women, by invitation, to the theatre for the two days. Some had never seen the inside of a theatre, and the architecture cowed them. But, once inside, the theatre tyros relaxed as the hairdressers and make-up experts taught them to look as well-groomed, glamorous and elegant as their business clients. During the rest of the day, they did role plays that required them to play their own and their customers' parts. At night, their own families welcomed them home in their new elegant looks. The next day at the theatre they dabbled in their new make-up and coiffure skills and ran through difficult simulations with customers. The training gave these front-liners a 'big boost'. Sodexho's management received thank you notes from the participants telling them how the training had improved their lives – work *and* family.

Retain

Employee and client retention are key to profitability. The two are inextricably linked. All service companies know that many, if not all clients will walk out if the service they get leaves them dissatisfied. One of the most common causes of service client defection is high levels of employee turnover at the site. So, Compass Group, Group 4 Falck, Securitas and Sodexho invest enormous amounts of time, money and management attention in retaining their staff. The four companies have extensive incentive programmes linked to individual or company performance.

Sodexho aligns its remuneration policies with the main ways it aims to create value. Depending on options, between 10% and 50% of a manager's annual bonus objectives is tied to the company's most important indicators of operational performance. Employee stock ownership plans (ESOPs), since their introduction in 1993, have proven very popular with Sodexho employees, since they demonstrate the Group's commitment to motivating employees by enabling them to share in its growth and financial performance. From 23 April to 27 July 2001, Sodexho opened its capital to 150 000 employees in 22 countries. In what it calls the 'Alliance' international employee stock ownership plan, all employees of Sodexho majority owned subsidiaries, *regardless of the employee's position in the organization*, could buy shares. 'Alliance Plus' allowed employees to invest up to 2.5% of their gross annual salary, with the possibility of leveraging any increase in the share price. 'Alliance Classic', however, allowed employees to invest up to 25% of their gross annual salary. These investors would receive the full capital gain from any increase in the share price, but would also incur the risk of decline. Regardless of the chosen option, employees may not sell shares for five years, except under certain conditions set out by law. Even better news for Sodexho employees is that the company not only offers up its shares at a deep discount but, according to Pierre Bellon, Alliance Plus offers them an equity stake in the company *at no risk*. 'We guarantee the initial capital, but if there is a capital gain, they can have a part of the capital gain.' In all, some 19 000 employees purchased 1 385 848 shares at a unit price of €41.51, with each participant taking an average of 75 shares (82% took Alliance Plus; 6% Alliance Classic; 12% a combination of both). Since 1993, when Sodexho introduced employee stock ownership plans, more than 32 000 employees have taken on an aggregate 1.74% of the company's capital.

In Finland the turnover of Sodexho's managerial staff is 3%, which is 7% lower than the industry average, and well below the restaurant business in general. Kirsti Piponius sees several reasons for the low figures:

Firstly, because we are extremely careful whom we hire, and after this we take care the job is interesting and people have the possibility to develop and make a career. It is also important that we don't compromise on quality . . . we simply are a good company! We also have some benefits that our competitors don't have. We have a bonus system for everyone. A waitress, for example, can make an extra month's salary per year.

Kirsti Piponius, Managing Director, Sodexho Finland

Compass Group also gives employees the opportunity to own part of the business: 32 000 employees in Compass Group are currently included in a share programme; among them 2000 management option holders. Explains Francis Mackay:

We have 'incentivized' people very heavily with share options and long-term incentive schemes . . . about 5% of the company is owned by employees and management. We have made our shareholders very, very wealthy. We have created huge shareholder value. Share schemes represent a huge commitment for a company like ours. Take our Group as an example, with 300 000 employees, it needs a much bigger share option capacity than a company in, say, shipping which has all its investments in assets and can handle their business with 200 people. Successful people need to be well-rewarded, not just in a good salary, but a good capital development.

Francis Mackay, Chairman, Compass Group

At Securitas, the group of branch managers responsible for profit centres (as of 2002, the 2000-strong group was still growing) is a key to success, so the company tries to retain them with extensive incentive schemes. Rewarding performance – and informing the wider organization of its people's successes – sends a message down through the company about what matters. But employees get a slice of the pie, too. When Securitas went public in 1991, every employee had the chance to buy in. Out of 5000, about 3000 did. In 2001, employees and managers owned about 5% of Securitas. Many of them were guards, and they made a lot of money.

A lot of guards bought for 100 000 Swedish Kroner. So if the share is up 25 times, that's millions, if they kept their shares. We offered something that is very popular nowadays – convertible loans where you actually loan the company money and later get your money back, or more preferably, you get stock back after a certain period. If the stock has moved up, you get back a much higher value than the initial

*loan. We have never said, 'If you're on this level you get this much, and if you're
on that level, you get that much.'*

Thomas Berglund, CEO, Securitas

Group 4 Falck's John Dueholm acknowledges that a fair salary is an
important factor in retaining staff:

*In order to attract the right people and to keep them, we see to it that their average
salaries are in the upper quartile compared with the industry. In countries like
Finland, Sweden, Norway, Denmark, the Baltic Countries and Poland we have
been very active in increasing guards' salaries in the market in general.*

*John Dueholm, former COO of Group 4 Falck
and as of 1 September 2002, Executive Vice President SAS,
Scandinavian Airline Systems*

Dueholm also says that owning a part of the company, however small,
creates a much higher level of employee interest in the well-being of the
company as a whole. More than 9000 employees currently own shares in
Group 4 Falck A/S.

*The fact that employees have shares and options makes it easier to communicate
and translate the value drivers. This has an effect on the share price, including the
employees' share price. I will bet that 80% of those who have shares often look at
the share price and the profit we make.*

*John Dueholm, former COO of Group 4 Falck
and as of 1 September 2002, Executive Vice President SAS,
Scandinavian Airline Systems*

In addition to a sweet package of salaries and benefits, the chance to
make a career is one of the most important reasons people will want to stay
with a service company. The four companies promote managers from
inside, and offer copious opportunities for professional growth and
advancement, both nationally and internationally.

Compass Group: Endless career opportunities

Gary Green, a dyed-in-the-wool Compass Group man, started his career at
the Goliath of food service as an accountant. 'I was going to be a "whiz kid"',

he recalls, wryly. 'I planned to stay two years and then do something else.' But Green couldn't bring himself to leave. Instead he found himself on the express escalator in a company that some sharp finance people were putting together. Green woke up from his whiz kid dream to discover that his ability to immerse himself in the numbers and in the operational side had suddenly earned him a shot at being Michael J. Bailey's CFO when Bailey was tagged as Compass Group's CEO in North America. Only half a decade later, Green was the natural next-in-line for the North American CEO position.

> *No other company in the United States can offer employees the breadth of food service career options we can. The only reason someone would leave our company is that we fail to recognize him or her. There is no room for big egos [at Compass Group]. We strive to be humble and not let ourselves get carried away by our success.*[3]
>
> Gary Green, CEO, Compass North America

The experience of Compass Group restaurant supervisor mirrors Green's:

> *I think there are no limits in this company, in theory I can become country manager if I want to. When my boss went on a training session, he gave the chef and me the responsibility over the administration of the restaurant, normally his job. This testifies to a lot of confidence in us in that we are taking care of a very large and important client with lots of relationships in the business world. He could have called in an interim manager – we have them, they're like members of a flying squad that come and fill in for managers on absence. But he did not.*
>
> Restaurant supervisor, Compass Group

As Mackay says, Compass Group doesn't just reward people for good performance and give them a shot at the next step up the company ladder, it also makes a culture of thanking people for a job well done, expressing appreciation openly and generously. When one of Compass Group's sales directors in the United States and the rest of his team won a large IBM contract, Francis Mackay invited them all over to London, with their wives, and 'took care of them'. Mackay wined and dined them in what is now the only Michelin three-star restaurant in the United Kingdom, and

---

[3]   Lawn, John, 'Multiple brands serving a single vision', *Food Management*, Cleveland, September 2001.

then trundled them off to a show – a wonderful evening for all. This was on top of a generous financial reward.

> *The real issue was around rewarding them for a wonderful job done. It was the beginning of a process, so it was important to send a message to everybody. This is important – people look for signals ... how am I going to be successful in this group? What is seen as success? Success was winning major contracts like that.*
> Francis Mackay, Chairman, Compass Group

Sodexho: Up the company ladder

When Albert George was appointed CEO of Sodexho, he had been with the company for more than 30 years. He had joined just after getting his first degree in economics. He was first recruited after an interview with Pierre Bellon in a taxi. His very first task was organizing a number of Sodexho sites: first in southern France, then in the Greater Paris area. He learned the day-to-day ins and outs of the food service business – how to manage inventory slips and stock levels and helped implement management tools that are still used today, for example a daily cost-price system. Over time, he became involved in almost all Sodexho activities:

> *During my years at Sodexho I have had some very exciting experiences that have helped me improve enormously. My multi-faceted career has enabled me to change jobs without changing companies, to constantly enhance my skills and benefit from an extremely rewarding international experience.*
> Albert George, CEO, Sodexho Alliance

Wherever possible, Sodexho tries to promote internally:

> *We look outside the company only in cases where there is no other option. I think it is good and is probably what brings the consistency of philosophy at Sodexho.*
> Patrice Douce, retired COO, Sodexho Alliance

A senior manager in the Universal Sodexho operations in Middle East, Asia and North East Africa, received 22 recognitions, either through promotion or in the form of a pay rise, during his 21 years of service in the group.

> *I made my debut with Sodexho group in Iraq as a fresh graduate in 1981, in the position of waiter. I spent 15 months on one of the remote sites in Iraq, and gained*

hands-on experience in various positions: Food and Beverages service, Food production, Housekeeping/Laundry/Store Management and Camp Management. Then a Human Resources Manager took me on as a 'Trainee Personnel Officer'. From then on I followed intensive training in the Human Resources Department, and was transferred to Finance and Accounting in Sodexho Oman. After gaining enough knowledge and experience I was given the responsibility of Human Resources Department with manpower strength of 388 employees. Due to the steep business growth in subsequent years, I was managing a total of 1427 employees at the time of my promotion and transfer to another senior position in 1997.

Manager, Sodexho Middle East

Since internal promotion is a group priority at Sodexho, it's not at all surprising that one staff member who began his career with the company as the Shanghai office chief became Central China Regional Director in 1999 in recognition of a sustained performance that began with a first major contract in 1995. The team in the subsidiary, which has a 50% growth rate and excellent client retention, is exclusively Chinese, and today is 1000 strong, working on 50 sites, of which one-quarter offers multiservices. A Senior Operations Manager in the Middle East started his career as an Assistant Cook in 1979. When he showed interest in camp management, his boss offered him intensive training in operations management, and after he had gained experience, subsequently gave him the opportunity to manage a camp of 1000 people of three nationalities. He has since worked as Purchasing Manager, General Service Department Manager and Operations Manager.

Group 4 Falck: With the right attitude you can become anything

If you're a fire-fighter with the municipality of Copenhagen, you work for the fire department. You get to the office at 8, eat, do some fitness training, sleep from one to three, do a little monkey business, then you sit by the TV and watch for the rest of your shift, only interrupted by the calls. You are a fire fighter from now until you retire. Fire fighting is exciting and important, but with Falck, you can become a paramedic and drive the ambulance, and if you get tired of that, you can take two fire fighting shifts. If you get tired of fire fighting and driving the ambulance, you can drive a tow truck and listen to all the people's stories about why they crashed. Or you can drive animals – save kittens from trees and ducklings from the pond. You could even be a chauffeur on one of our surveillance teams. Whatever!

Johnny Eikeland, Group 4 Falck

Very often, shop stewards develop into managers, particularly in The Netherlands, and often the training there is done in the local unions. That's one of our important recruitment pools. But today I would think it's not likely that you go all the way from being a rescuer or a guard to become the CEO. But you can go pretty far up the hierarchy to become a divisional manager or a branch manager or something like that and a lot of people do. At the first three or four operational levels we almost only rely on internal recruitment from people who have had experience being a rescuer or a guard.

Lars Nørby Johansen, CEO, Group 4 Falck

In 1994, when Group 4 took over the fire brigade at Opel Austria, Austrian Dietmar Ottahal had a simple choice: stay at Opel Austria, where he had been shift manager of the Opel fire brigade, leave Opel, or become a member of the Group 4 team. Dietmar had a long conversation with Group 4 managing director, Stephan Landrock, and 'soon knew what to do'. He went with Group 4.

This decision was the right one for several reasons. First of all, our team is a good and sympathetic one: when I joined the company I felt at home immediately. Secondly, Group 4 offers you many possibilities of making a career. Today I am the leader of all static guards in Vienna. I am concerned with matters of customer care, but I am also still – and I wouldn't want to miss it – commander of the Group 4 Falck fire brigade.

Dietmar Ottahal, Static Guards Leader in Vienna, Group 4 Falck

---

**JOHNNY EIKELAND – INTERNAL CAREER
GROUP 4 FALCK**

1971	Rescuer, with one year on-the-job training
	Third person on ambulances
1970s	Further training
	Starts ambulance service on Rhodes, Greece
1980s	Writes articles for Falck's internal magazines on US approach to rescue operations
1985	Employed in business development department
1990	Employed in internal communications department
2001	Elected employee representative on G4F board

Brian Avril started in 1965 at Group 4 Total Security as a mobile patrol officer, or 'beatman'. A bad car accident on duty led to a transfer into static guarding at Carlos Place in London, to start and run the control centre. From there, he progressed to being the youngest operational superintendent ever and took over responsibility for alarm monitoring. In November 1971 he was appointed assistant manager of the North London division. In a few months, he became divisional manager (1975). Two years later, he was made training manager, and after three years in that position, the company asked him to fill the vacant position of regional general manager for London, with responsibility for the alarms company, cash-in-transit, retail and guarding services as well as sales and personnel. In 1981, he was appointed to the commercial development division, and then, two years later, he became director of Euroguard a new division of the guarding company. The year 1987 saw him become the company's first director of quality, which led, a decade later, to his becoming Group director of quality. An unusual career at Group 4 Falck? No, and not so unusual at the other three companies either.

It is not only the star performers who ride the track to job satisfaction at Group 4 Falck. Those who do not wish to make such meteoric careers are also tracked for job satisfaction in Group 4 Falck:

> Four times a year everybody is asked to complete an employee satisfaction questionnaire. We follow up on problems in specific departments. For example, it could be that there is no dialogue with the manager. Generally, we analyse how the cooperation between employee and manager works and – if it does not work – the reason why. Nursing your personnel is one of the most important things in a service company. And if you as a manager score low on one of the parameters in the questionnaire, you will have a negative impact on our relation to customers. We then will define action plans for how to improve and we follow up in the next employee satisfaction programme.
>
> John Dueholm, former COO of Group 4 Falck
> and as of 1 September 2002, Executive Vice President SAS,
> Scandinavian Airline Systems

Securitas: Increasing job satisfaction and developing staff

> If you start as a guard, how far can you go in Securitas? Well, my job.
> Thomas Berglund, CEO, Securitas

In California, Securitas has reorganized to create some vertical segments (one branch manager manages the retailers in the area) and some geographic units (a town, for example). This means that a branch manager in a town has to become part of the community, meeting the chief of police and the members of the fire department, learning the local ordinances. 'The branch managers reacted very positively' to this change, says Tony Sabatino, Area Manager, Securitas USA.

> *It saves them time, they have a smaller region, a flatter structure, more time to focus on clients. Once you become part of a community and you understand your clients better, then you get more job satisfaction. So we are seeing lower turnover. I haven't lost one yet! One manager left to go to a local family-based competitor as she missed the 'family atmosphere', but she came back in 10 days because she really missed our professional environment.*
>
> Tony Sabatino, Area Manager, Securitas USA

> *Staff turnover at our unit is lower than the turnover of staff at other security firms because of the way we treat people and the autonomy we give them. Since we have been able to raise the wages, recruiting is easier and turnover has stabilized. In theory the salaries of guards at our competitors should have been raised as well, but we have noticed that not all security companies have the same level of integrity as Securitas. In some companies the guards are not paid for their working hours according to present legislation.*
>
> Chantal Austin, Regional Manager, Securitas Normandy, France

There are many examples of internal careers at Securitas. Many guards or other front-line employees have indeed achieved management positions. Look at the story of the country president for Norway. During his 25 years at Securitas, Bjørn Lohne has tramped the steep path from service engineer to Country President for Norway. On 22 March 1976 Lohne began as a service engineer, as much a coincidence as anything else that it was at Securitas. For five years he worked as an engineer, but in 1981, he became the foreman of the service department, a slot he held for another six years. In 1987, however, he made a big step up to installation manager, and then, a year later, another big step to technical manager for Norway's eastern region, shouldering responsibilities he held until 1991. During that intense period, he was also sub-branch manager of a Hedmark (Norway) office for six months. When the six-month sub-branch stint ended, Lohne went back to being the technical manager, but only until August. Securitas had bigger things in mind for him: Technical Director for Securitas Norway, the position he has held the longest – but no longer holds. As of September 2000, he became Country President, and in 2002, Divisional President Security Systems USA.

> *Each country has its way of doing things, but ultimately the principles for creating change and motivation towards profitability are basically the same. I'm most proud of the 'developing and blossoming' of the people in the organization as they have begun to realize that there are excellent career opportunities at Securitas.*
>
> Bjørn Lohne, Country President Securitas, Norway

Build partnerships with unions and works councils

Compass Group and Sodexho

THE SODEXHO APPROACH TO UNIONS

In France and countries such as Germany it's the law to work with the unions. No option. So either you say 'too bad' or you say, 'How can we take advantage of this?' As we deal with a lot of people and there is nothing to be hidden in our actions, the more we explain what we do and why we do it the more support we get from the staff, including the unionized people. I think unions have changed significantly in 30 years. I think unions tend to be more responsible now. We have always chosen good communication, open communication rather than confronting the unions.

Patrice Douce, retired COO, Sodexho

Faced with a wide array of options for changing the industry from a place where unskilled labourers with little or no training get the minimum wage to prepare and serve food into one where skilled and well-trained workers are proud to say they work for Compass Group or Sodexho, both companies chose to work hand-in-hand with the unions to improve basic pay for front-line employees and make individual jobs more attractive to prospective employees.

Mackay takes a 'pragmatic' and 'constructive' view of unions. Not surprisingly, Compass Group sees them as 'partners'. The one area, says

Mackay, where Compass Group had the greatest difficulty, was 'getting the works council introduced in the United Kingdom, where, historically, perhaps unions were far more aggressive than in the rest of Europe'. But by 2002, after five years of working with the unions, the partnership is part of Compass Group human resources development. 'We get them to help us lead. We give them, say, three months to think about certain issues. They come back and say, "Well, we've looked at this, and we think the way forward is such and such". We work together. It isn't confrontational. We use the unions, and they are happy for us to do that.'

Securitas

Berglund comes back to his service-is-people argument to explain his wish to foster good relations with unions and works councils:

> This is a business about people and to develop people. The service you deliver can never be better than the people you hire. If you can, over five to 10 years, raise the wage levels substantially, you can attract a substantially different group of people, and that, in turn, improves your ability to develop your people – and your business.
>
> Thomas Berglund, CEO, Securitas

Securitas has a 'very good relation to the unions' because the company is known as a tireless supporter of wage development. Andrew Stern, President of SEIU (Service Employees International Union), recalls how Securitas worked with the unions after the terrorist attacks of 11 September 2001. Compared with some of its competitors, Securitas only had a small stake in the airport security business, nevertheless it wanted to collaborate with the unions to achieve better working conditions for airport screeners and security personnel in general so they could attract and keep better staff and so that their service would be safer:

> The US Congress debated the future of the screening industry, whether it would be federal or private. All the Security CEOs were in the country trying to understand what was going on and what would happen to their industry. Berglund was the only one who came to see me. All the others, including the American CEOs, would not meet with me, even though their business was at stake and even though we were

agreeing with them on many of the principles. Berglund was the one who tried to form a partnership with the others and to come and talk to us together. He failed initially; not many turned up at the meeting. This embarrassed Berglund. He even had to drag his own (acquired) managers to the meeting. In the end I think he convinced them that union people did have something to offer and that not talking to people for historic reasons was not on. He tried to create a different relationship, not dwell on our old relationship. I think he did give the managers a new perspective . . . that we are stronger together.

Andrew Stern, President SEIU, USA

Group 4 Falck

Sørensen of Group 4 Falck actually goes so far as to *thank* the unions. 'One of the best things I have had in my baggage is my Scandinavian experience. In Scandinavia there has for many years been a tradition where companies work together with unions, where you have, as a company, in principle at least, the same philosophy as the unions: you like people to be well-paid, to be trained, to be respected for what they do.' Can a security company apply the same principles in any country anywhere? Of course not. 'You have to tailor-make it and manage it within the framework of the culture of the particular country – you cannot just copy Danish or Swedish systems. That won't work.' Sorensen claims a lesson he learned from working with the unions was, 'when you talk to the labour force, you show them that not only your products are unique, but that also the way you manage your people is unique.'

Nørby Johansen, CEO of Group 4 Falck, agrees: 'I have long had the attitude that strong unions are good for a company but it takes strong management. It's very synergetic when strong unions go together with strong management.' Nørby Johansen's priority is to keep working through the Group 4 Falck network of unions in Europe through various cooperative committees, European Works council included: Nørby Johansen is Chairman.

It's one of the jobs I would not delegate to anyone else. I happen to be the symbol of the management of the company. I love it. I get very important input here. For me it's key to hear how our people think, their attitude to the rules, and a number of things that I don't normally hear through the management system, because the information is quite often 'selected' down to whatever people think I would like to hear, not what I need to hear.

Lars Nørby Johansen, President and CEO, Group 4 Falck

THE SWEDISH MODEL

When unions, security contractors, trade organizations and police authorities work side by side, the results can be outstanding. Such is the case in Sweden where several examples of cooperation have led to extremely low turnover of staff – between 5% and 10% – and an average wage for security guards that is on par with industrial workers.

Together with Almega, the association of security company employers and Svenska Transportarbetareförbundet, the guards union, established the Swedish Institute for Guard Training in 1997. Here, 5200 students from any of the country's 300 security companies undergo 217 hours of basic training within their first six months of employment. Basic training includes technology and computer skills, ethics, fire prevention and fire fighting, familiarity with legal matters, rescue techniques, CPR training, service and conflict management.

The Institute also provides specialized training in group leadership and courses for shop guards or cash-in-transit guards. In its efforts to gain a broader base for recruitment, the industry is now setting its sights on establishing training at the high-school level. Sweguard, the Swedish trade association, in a joint effort with the Institute and the union, is evaluating the possibility of establishing a two- or three-year high-school programme for guards-to-be.

Questions for service leaders

1. What key characteristics are you looking for in employees? Are these qualities truly reflected in all recruiting processes?

2. Are your orientation programmes effective enough to quickly integrate new employees into your company culture? Do they give an

understanding of the core elements of the business model (in addition to basic functional training)? How can you make them more effective?

3. Do your training programmes go well beyond the letter of the law? Are they designed to boost service attitude, encourage employees to take initiative and bolster the understanding of central corporate values? Do you heavily involve senior executives as 'faculty'?

4. Is promotion from inside the company a key strategy at all levels of the company? Are you utilizing the entire organization for developing managers by, for example, transferring and promoting high potential managers across unit/geographical borders?

5. Are your remuneration policies aligned with your key value creation drivers? Do you have incentive schemes that enable a large portion of your employees to feel responsible for company performance?

6. Do you view your relationships with unions, work councils or other employee representatives as an important value creation enhancer? How could you improve these relationships?

6

Keep it simple

Running a company is not science. If it were, it would be too expensive. We have to find the right short cuts and that means: keep it simple and do not over-complicate. All business is simple.

Thomas Berglund, CEO, Securitas

Many public and private organizations run on the premise that more control, more procedures and more labour adds up to better service. Not so Compass Group, Group 4 Falck, Securitas and Sodexho. The four companies believe that people will perform well if their employers offer them a decent job with fair pay and proper training, and respect them for their work. The four service giants want every employee to be accountable for providing their customers with the services they want and need, at the agreed cost. They believe, unanimously, that an especially good way to make employees accountable is to give them responsibility. And the way to farm out responsibility, at least in their service industries, is to design their organizations in a 'simple' way that rests responsibility in the hands of the people nearest the front line. How does this consciously simple company structure correlate with company success? What, specifically, do the four companies do to make their 1 000 000 employees take their responsibility? Simply put, they keep their hierarchy as simple as possible (*flat organization*) and put the responsibility for financial results, people management and customer service into the hands of branch managers or site managers (*decentralized decision-making*).

> ## SIMPLICITY AT SECURITAS
>
> An important part of Securitas' philosophy is to make workflows and the organization as simple as possible. This makes them clear and easy to follow. Simplicity also creates quality. Instructions should be easy to read and understand, alarm systems should be easy to install, and managers should be within easy reach of customers. When a task is completed in the simplest way possible, it will be done faster and smoother and produce better results.
>
> ***People Make the Difference, Securitas brochure***

More specifically, Compass Group, Group 4 Falck, Securitas and Sodexho believe in the value of front-line performance and direct interaction with customers, and, at the same time, they dislike large central functions and overhead layers that float far from the customer interface. None has a complicated matrix organization. Although their offices dot the globe, they operate with few management layers. Communication between front-line employees and people at the 'top' is as direct as the companies can make it. Our four companies decentralize responsibility and decision-making more than many industrial companies and competing service organizations. They farm out as many activities as they can to individual country organizations and business units. Profit and loss and customer responsibility accrue to branch and restaurant managers. The lines of communication from the top management to those in the company uniforms are short and direct. They also have created *small head offices* that focus only on the areas that require central control (e.g. group accounting) and where obvious advantages exist in central coordination (e.g. purchasing, legal). Even these departments are small and run with few bells and whistles. Where the companies have had to create processes, they have tried to keep them austere and streamlined.

Flat organization and decentralized decision-making

The four companies believe in keeping their organizations simple, transparent and relatively flat. The organizational set-up varies from one company to the next, from geographical to business line organizations. In all four, vertical compression ensures not only that they can allocate management capacity and other resources to the front line with maximum efficiency, but also that information flows vertically and transparently. In all four cases, comparatively few management levels separate the CEO from front-line employees. In their flat 'empowered' organizations, Compass Group, Group 4 Falck, Securitas and Sodexho have 8–15 people reporting to one. Many companies in the service industry have a maximum of eight people reporting to 1. The transparent organization enables the senior management team to quickly get messages, for example about vision, strategy, or values, to all employees. It also ensures that the CEO and other top managers have a good overview of the true performance of different operating units.

Sodexho

At any site, the site manager reports to the regional manager who reports to the country manager. And the country manager, sometimes specialized in a segment, is one of the 150 managers who are part of the senior management team that sets our strategy.

Member of the senior management team, Sodexho Alliance

Sodexho has 24 300 sites in 72 countries. Every site has, on average, 12–13 employees. Each and every one is informed of the company's direction; each has a card printed with the company's mission, objectives, and core values.

Compass Group

Compass Group separates brands and units for different activities, be they corporate dining, school catering, roadside food services, vending or even upscale dining.

We have individual brand names and teams such as Eurest, Medirest, Scolarest, and Select Service Partner so they can each own their own business, and that has been a very important motivator for capturing the best management.

Francis Mackay, Chairman, Compass Group

This separation gives Compass Group managers the feeling of being 'entrepreneurs' with a personal sense of responsibility for the numbers that show up in the columns of the quarterly profit and loss statements.

Group 4 Falck

Group 4 Falck arranges its management geographically. According to Nels Petersen:

> *Normally, if you take Sweden, for example, you have one management team, one CEO (sometimes we call them managing directors) who is responsible for all the accounts in Sweden, across the map. Then you have a director for each of the different kinds of business: ambulance services, guarding, alarms, and they are part of the management team for the country, in this case, Sweden. Underneath you have regions or districts, and within them, the sites, each with a site manager.*
> *Nels Petersen, Group Communications Director, Group 4 Falck*

Group 4 Falck has six layers in its organization: CEO, Region Manager, Function Manager, Branch Manager, Team Leader and Security Guard. No need for a Master's degree in flow engineering to know who's doing what. It's simple and clear.

Securitas

The Securitas blueprint is based on functional building blocks, instead of being drawn along geographical lines, in order to concentrate on each segment. Securitas' organization has as few decision-making levels as possible. The company says this optimizes quality, efficiency and motivation of employees. Within each country, Securitas divides its organization into areas, which in turn consist of a number of branch offices that operate as independent profit centres. The company's goal is never to have more than three layers between the guard or service technician and the country president. The country president, in turn, reports to a divisional president, who reports to the CEO.

With more than 230 000 employees, Securitas has five management levels, while its competitors with fewer than 50 000 employees often operate with seven to eight levels. From the CEO to a guard, Securitas, like Group 4 Falck, has only six organizational layers: CEO, Division Manager, Country Manager, Branch Manager, Team Leader and Guard. Securitas has 2000 profit centres, about 100 employees and €3 million in turnover per profit centre.

Securitas trusts its people to do the right thing for their customers, which means that it freely delegates responsibility to the operators and their 2000 managers.

> We have a lot of small units, very close to customers, with a lot of authority to make decisions and to deliver to those customers.
>
> Thomas Berglund, CEO, Securitas

The consequence, however, is that Securitas has to continuously provide front-liners and their bosses with the necessary knowledge, skills and confidence to take responsibility.

Securitas believes that its success relates directly to its efficient operations and, in Berglund's words, 'the way we have organized...many small units, very close to customers, with a lot of authority to take decisions and deliver to those customers'. Consider the stark contrast between the Securitas organization and that of Pinkerton, one of its major acquisitions (besides Burns) in the United States:

> Pinkerton's once grand corporate office of a thousand staff is now referred to as its support services centre. In Pinkerton, the lawyers and accountants and other staff functions made policy decisions. In Securitas, line management makes those types of decisions. And that is a big difference. Pinkerton had more of a dictatorial top management. Burns was a little more decentralized, and Securitas is dramatically more decentralized.
>
> Tony Sabatino, Area Manager, Securitas

The Securitas flat structure actually motivates people, believes Torben Sand, financial analyst, Svenska Handelsbanken, Copenhagen. 'The whole decentralized structure actually incentivizes people to take on responsibility'. By following this concept of decentralizing (and flattening the organization), Securitas now has a very broad management team – many highly-skilled, local managers, right down to the branch level.

According to Sand, this is not something that was invented a few years back, 'this has been the core of Securitas' strategy since the "modern" Securitas started in the mid-1980s'.

EMPOWERMENT IN A FLAT ORGANIZATION
Gunela Juninger, Group Leader,
Stockholm Globe Arena (Securitas)

Securitas has been guarding the Stockholm Globe Arena since December 1989. Gunela Juninger started work at Securitas in 1984, as a guard when she was a student, and has been on the Globe Arena project since day one. Three Securitas employees work at the Stockholm Globe Arena during the day, two at night. During the events season, when activity peaks, four employees do the day shifts. The work is carried out by a static security guard, a mobile patrol guard, an administrator and Gunela. They handle all duties associated with a guard control centre: access control for people, vehicles and transports, goods reception, visitor reception, door and gate control, lighting control, monitoring, handling alarms, and more. Early on she was a so-called 'Group Leader', but now she is a Group Leader with customer responsibility, a 'new concept' that brings added – and welcome – responsibilities to group leaders.

Having been on the project for more than 10 years, Gunela came to know the ins and outs of guarding the arena very well. She always had a close relationship with the customer – she calls it a 'partnership' – but she always felt that her powers were limited because she lacked the authority to do what was required. The customers discussed their concerns with her, but she 'didn't have access to the contract' and therefore didn't know its precise contents. This made it difficult for her to discuss issues or justify Securitas' activities with the customer. When the customer had a question, Gunela had to say she needed to talk to her boss before getting back to them. A few times each year, a couple of gentlemen from Securitas came to negotiate prices. For the customer, Gunela knew, 'this didn't feel right...the customer had no relationship with these gentlemen, who, in turn, found it difficult to justify, argue in favour of and gain the customers' sympathy for price increases for an object they knew far less about than Gunela. The customer wanted Gunela as their contact person, and wanted Securitas to grant her the additional authority.

'This customer has been a driving force in our efforts to introduce the Group Leader with customer responsibility concept, without really knowing it', says Gunela. But since Securitas claims to listen to the customer, the company had 'to adapt its operations'. Now, Gunela 'owns the contract', can see every aspect of the business and can work with the customer to improve service and gain more business for Securitas. The advantages? 'When you actually work at a customer site on a daily basis, you naturally build up a sense of mutual confidence, and the customer knows that you have really understood what the assignment entails', says Gunela. 'Now I can solve issues directly with the customer, on site, without having to go to my boss...quality has improved and things go faster and easier now that I have the authority to solve problems and propose actions myself'. There's no question that my job is more fun now, working with the business, selling and producing better results. The difference is that now I'm the one who sells and prices our services. When you handle finances for yourself, and can actually see the figures, selling is fun. Our extra guarding services have increased dramatically, and I can now personally initiate and propose extra guarding and other measures more easily than before. And when it comes to price negotiations, for example, it's obviously easier for me to argue in favour of a price increase because I'm on the site and know what's involved.

Small head office

To Compass Group, Group 4 Falck, Securitas and Sodexho, a big HQ is an obstacle to an active, customer-oriented organization. With bloated HQs, they assume, a company risks binding its site or branch managers to their offices. This top-heavy centralization is not for our four companies. Three have head offices with fewer than 50 people; Sodexho, the exception, boasts 100, which is still much smaller than the HQs for most organizations with over 300 000 employees.

The small HQs of the industry leaders are strictly 'no frills', with critical functions only. They are kept small as part of the philosophy of decentralized decision-making. Our four companies do not believe that bureaucrats in a remote head office make the best decisions. They believe that as many decisions as possible must be pushed out to the front line. The 'operations' are empowered, not the head office. To them, a network of many small local 'head offices' seems to be the best architecture. The real 'centre' of the organization, as contradictory as it may seem, is not one building somewhere in a major metropolis, but rather in each of the thousands of sites and branches where front-liners and branch managers organize and offer some of the world's best security and food services.

Sodexho

Sodexho places management responsibility in the capillaries of its circulatory system. The company puts the responsibility for growth in the regions and segments with its middle managers, who it sees as entrepreneurs in the style of Pierre Bellon. The main task of the 200-strong Sodexho corporate head office in Paris is to chisel out a global strategy, with the 150 top managers lending a hand. Managing the company's finances, especially financial control and investments, is the second task. A third is communication: from the head office the company tries to 'educate the sites on how to communicate with their groups'. The quality management processes are an example.

SODEXHO: LINKING TOP AND FRONT LINE IN A STRATEGY CREATING PROCESS

To make the link from top management out to the front line, the top 150 managers have worked with the senior executive team to create a reference book called *Corporate Strategic Orientations*, built on the same ideas as the employee cards. The *Corporate Strategic Orientations* is a working document that contains the strategic directions for the company over the next three years, but that is also adapted every year in a three-day meeting of the same 150 top managers. Once the top 150 agree that the document provides the right direction to the more than 24 000 sites around the world, it goes out into the organization via the next management layer. The 150 work with their direct reports, who have, in turn, worked with their managers, to write a three-year strategic plan and a one-year budget. The idea is that managers involve their staff in creating their plans, in the same way as Sodexho's executive committee has involved them in creating the strategic orientation. This ensures consistency and transparency throughout the organization and, at the same time, provides managers with the room to empower their staff. Initiatives are much appreciated as long as they fall within the boundaries agreed on in the strategic orientation.

Pierre Bellon has always emphasized that the head office should contain few but very competent people. Often members of staff come to him to try to convince him they need more staff, but the answer is usually 'No! Take someone from the outside on a temporary, consulting basis.' We don't mind hiring consultants as much as we mind adding staff to the structure.

An employee of the Sodexho head office

Compass Group

Compass Group maintains a very small corporate headquarters: about 60 people. Virtually all of the necessary resources are clustered in the head offices of each of its 96 countries of operation. The US head office in Charlotte, North Carolina, has 400 people; Paris, the hub of the French company, has 250 people. At the centre of the Compass Group galaxy of country constellations is its Southern England based corporate headquarters, which has finance, tax, treasury, corporate relations, corporate communication and an HR team that coordinates HR processes and oversees the strategic direction.

So what we have, at the centre is a coordination of processes. We don't direct anything from [the centre], because it would be impossible. With 360 000 people, if we were trying to manage the business from there, we would need 4000 people at the centre. Impossible . . . and also the wrong way around, since the resources need to be in each of the countries where the business is, near the front line.

Francis Mackay, Chairman, Compass Group

Group 4 Falck

A head office should be as small as possible, although there are certain functions you must have [there], particularly if you are a public company.

J. Philip-Sørensen, Chairman of the Board of Directors, Group 4 Falck

J. Philip-Sørensen of Group 4 Falck suggests, albeit tongue-in-cheek, that there are actually thousands of company headquarters in Group 4 Falck, since the *real* head offices are 'probably the branch offices where you have your guards and your supervisors, because that's where things really happen'. Sørensen clearly equates 'head office', by definition, with the place where the employees have the most contact with customers.

To Sørensen's way of thinking, a widely distributed network company like Group 4 Falck needs financial control at the centre. It needs legal minds to see that contracts are within the margins of the law and that the company doesn't leave itself open to legal dangers that would hurt employees and customers ('in that order' he exclaims). Headquarters keeps tabs on the Group's insurance coverage and also manages risk. HR policy and guidelines have their place in the centre – the branches recruit.

> *Overall staff policy must be maintained, because otherwise the local Chief Executive might make some fancy systems for his staff in one country that won't go in other countries . . . and then you're in a total mess.*
>
> J. Philip-Sørensen, Chairman of the Board of Directors, Group 4 Falck

Above all, suggests Sørensen, a service company needs in its small HQ a key figure who is in no way a frill: a CEO who is totally committed to the profession and to the company, supported by a highly motivated and skilled secretariat who are going to 'work like the clappers' while the CEO is out on the road.

Securitas

Securitas splits its head office among the three points of an imaginary triangle: Stockholm, London and Dublin. Seven book-keepers in the Swedish capital do the books for the consolidated group. From Dublin, seven staff take care of treasury, all the money and transactions, essentially funding the company's expansion. The CEO and his staff of 15 drive the business from a small office in London. Two work on investor relations, and another three work on internal relations, training included. Then there's legal, a couple of people helping with mergers and acquisitions, and a tax person. That makes a total of 35 people in the holding. 'You have to understand that it works because it is decentralized', says Thomas Berglund, 'thirty-five people cannot manage a company of more than 200 000 people.'

One step out into the country divisions are roughly 1000 people who have administrative functions. All the way into the branch 'reality' where a guard in a Securitas uniform shines a flashlight around a dark room at three am, says Berglund, 'we talk about 20 000 people doing overhead management and administration'.

Securitas gives the example of one of their US acquisitions, a large US security firm that had 1000 people at its California HQ. This hoard of central bureaucrats sent out instructions and policies and requests for information and asked for lots of reports. All the entries for the company book-keeping were made at the California headquarters. 'The British operation, for example, sent everything to California where the books were produced. Everything was top-down driven.' Branch managers felt chained to their offices, and had limited time only for customers and front-line staff.

> *A large head office does not only cost a lot of money but it has all the power, and that is more of a problem because the people in the field will just sit and wait for orders and they will be busy filling out reports. The whole drive will come from the head office and the people in the field will just react, not to the market but to the head office.*
> *Thomas Berglund, CEO, Securitas*

Compass Group, Group 4 Falck, Securitas and Sodexho are 'people-driven' rather than 'systems driven'. In their mind this is the only way you can successfully run and grow a service business with hundreds of thousands of people in thousands of sites across the world. They do not spend their time on rewriting strategic documents every quarter, they execute instead. They do not spend much time on writing manuals either. They run their businesses as groups of families where the examples are set by the heads of the families (be it the CEO or the supervisor at a site). When we asked Thomas Berglund whether Securitas is guided by manuals he replied: 'You don't write manuals for your kids, do you?'

Questions for service leaders

1. Can your organization make fast decisions at the front line while also securing overall direction-setting and control of the company's development?

2. How transparent is your organization? How long does it take for a senior executive to receive vital signals from customers? Do your front-line employees understand the key strategic thrusts of the company?

3. What would happen if one or two organizational layers were removed?

4. What decision-making and financial accountability rests with the managers far out in different branches/sites versus HQ staff?

5. Does the current level of decentralization stimulate all front-line managers to deliver customer service to their unit's full potential? Do they feel personally responsible for their unit's financial result?

6. Do all your head office functions fulfil tasks that can't be handled by individual business areas/business units?

7. What criteria do you use for deciding whether functions are best handled by the head office or by individual business units? Can you better balance your trade-offs between market closeness on the one hand, and scale, skill and control on the other hand?

7

Winning at service:
Final words

We wrote *Winning at Service: Lessons from Service Leaders* to help you – business leaders everywhere – realize the enormous potential of your companies. If you, together with your teams, decide to embark on a journey to leadership, the book, we hope, will help you draw up your route map; maybe spotlight some of the dangers and roadblocks you are likely to encounter; give you examples, ideas and concepts to increase your chances of getting successfully to where ever you may want to go. Remember, you don't have to lead the world, you can become a leader in a relevant geographical market or market segment. You don't have to employ hundreds of thousands of people to lead. Leadership is not about size, but about setting the trends and the standards in your industries. Overall size is not the key. Critical mass, significant 'market density' and market share in all your chosen markets and segments are key to being a real world leader.

As we worked on *Winning at Services*, we shared our research discoveries, namely that Compass Group, Group 4 Falck, Securitas and Sodexho took similar journeys to number one and two in their industries (we call it 'the journey to service leadership'), positions that had been held, for many years, by large US service companies. They outclassed tens of thousands of competitors, mostly small, local firms, and overtook – and later acquired – much larger rivals owned by powerful multinational conglomerates. They even bought US companies that once topped their industries.

Hearing these achievements, our listeners often argued that many, even *any* company could have achieved the same as Compass Group, Group 4

Falck, Securitas and Sodexho. To their surprise, our response was, 'This is exactly our point – many companies can win in the same way.' The leaders, seemingly surprised by their own success, claimed that their journeys to leadership have actually been simple ones. 'Luck', they say, 'we've been very very lucky.' With hindsight, the journey to service industry leadership *looks* pretty simple. But if it's so simple, why haven't more companies succeeded? The same tools are available to all; the same choices; the same potential. Why have so few of the tens of thousands of service companies out there surged ahead? You can't buck the evidence: very few make it. Only a select few even keep up with our four juggernauts. How come? Because the journey is not quite as simple as it appears – substantial barriers block the way. At every turn lurk dangers.

For one, winning at services means applying the principles, values and concepts in this book, not merely for a few quarters, or a year or two, under the guise of some new-fangled change or improvement programme, not merely applying a few tricks for a while, and then abandoning them for the next craze, or managerial sleight of hand. No, winning at service means applying these principles, values and concepts over the long haul – 10, 15, or 20 years – with persistence, will-power and patience.

All our companies have deeply rooted robust and lasting strategies in place. Their strategies are *company strategies*, not CEO *strategies*. The problem with the majority of companies is that they have strategies that change with every new CEO. Read the financial press about appointments of new CEOs. In 99% of the cases you will see that the new CEO will announce his or her strategy in the first 100 days. This has become a routine. Financial analysts and company management expect a new strategy with the new CEO. With an average 'life-time' of three to five years for CEOs in their jobs, it is no wonder that only a few companies become great companies.

Our listeners were right: *any* service company probably can achieve long-term success *if* it is prepared to embark on a journey lasting 15–20 years, as our four companies did in the mid-1980s, *if* it can find the right combination of tools and values.

To meet these dual challenges, a service company needs to have the right character and attitude – *mindset*, you might say. What do we mean by mindset? There are myriad definitions, and it is beyond our remit to sort them out. But here's a simple example of what we're driving at. What some people see as very simple, others see as extremely complex. The difference in perception can be a difference in mindset. Remember the wise old story about the water glass? Set a glass on the table. Pour water into it. Watch until it fills to the middle. Stop. Now ask a few passers-by what they see. 'Why, it's half empty', some say. 'Half-full', proclaim the others. Why the different perceptions? Mindset, some experts believe. Person A sees the glass through a 'negative lens', while person B takes a more positive – optimistic – view. Try lobbing a tough business problem at a group of managers. What happens? A few see it as a chance to fail. Others rejoice at their chance to succeed. The difference, in our view, is mindset.

Among those who see the challenges of the service business as an invitation to victory, many have the best of intentions and the most glorious of dreams. Some read the business weeklies or attend faddish management seminars, and soon afterwards, they've taken a few new ideas on board and are suddenly boasting of new-spun, winning visions. To paraphrase the old saw: good intentions alone are no guarantee of service success. Many managers lose focus. Even in the small group of 'glass-half-full' managers, too many lose sight of what really matters. In the service industry, they take detours around roadblocks on their journey to a new destination or, on the steep, slippery road, fall back, give up, or miss a curve. The leaders in this book have a positive mindset: they see a problem as 'a solution looking for a place to happen'. They prefer to stop at a roadblock, remove it, put solutions in place to avoid or overcome it the next time it pops up, and get on with the job, all the while encouraging a can-do mindset in their teams. They take no detours, hold their course and keep their goals in sight. Don't misunderstand: they are neither myopic nor inflexible. They do watch the landscape. And they do talk to people they meet on the way. They never lose sight of their business goals. This belief-in-the-cause, coupled with unrelenting focus and iron will, enables them, when they face a hurdle, to remove it, all the while never losing sight of the company mission and goals.

So what are the common roadblocks? People are the most critical ones. Only if you assemble and retain a winning team over a *very long time*, are you going to win at service. Constantly replacing key players will eventually poison the most healthy growth. It's no coincidence that our four companies marry managerial longevity and year-long double-digit growth. Acquiring companies is the easiest of all management disciplines; offer enough money, and most owners will sell you their company. Integrating and running the companies you acquire, that's another story – one of the most difficult of all management disciplines. Witness the high number of acquisition failures, the long list of managers who destroy shareholder value instead of creating it. Just read the acquisition proposals that managers write to their boards or owners: they are the stuff of unrequited dreams. Compass Group, Group 4 Falck, Securitas and Sodexho have demonstrated, on their flights to the top, beyond reasonable doubt, that they know how to identify, acquire, integrate and run the hundreds of companies they have purchased. How did they surmount the acquisition roadblock? All four companies work predominantly with local managers and teach them how to run the business the 'Securitas Way', 'The Group 4 Falck Way', the 'Compass Group Way' and the 'Sodexho Way'. They help them become as good as the best in the group.

Among the further dangers awaiting the future service winner are:

- the inability, in family-owned or family controlled businesses, to relinquish power (shares, for example) to non-family members;
- the urge, especially as a company reaches conglomerate proportions, to do too many things;
- the concomitant failure to stick to the company mission and vision over many years;
- company leaders who manage through the lens of one particular management discipline – marketing or finance, for example – instead of drawing on the full palette of disciplines;
- doing a poor job bringing other companies' non-core businesses into your own core and, most important;
- cultivating the wrong mindset – focusing more on systems than on people.

Even as they themselves built world-class service companies, all five have proved themselves remarkably proficient at executing their visions, which included buying the non-core businesses of large conglomerates and integrating them into their own operations, as core businesses, where they smashed all records they had set as marginalized, non-core divisions. All our leaders are widely skilled in the full range of management disciplines and avoid falling back on one particular area of management expertise, like marketing or accounting, to make strategic decisions. And all have the right mindset: people before systems.

Win by relinquishing power

Pick up any book on family business and you'll read that most family-owned companies stay small and local. Some become large but still local companies. Of these, few go farther. A popular explanation is that family business owners often balk at putting power in the hands of non-family executives. Some try repeatedly, but fail. We have seen a number of good, large service companies, most of which started as small, local family companies, import a non-family 'genius' CEO every second or third year, with less than desirable results. Such firms eventually drop out of the marathon to world leadership. But a small, select group of family-owned companies – think of Tetra Pak, Ikea, Lego, S.C. Johnson – hold up to 100% ownership and still complete the journey to world leadership. These exceptions generally have to clear what you might call the double hurdle of 'non-owner manager and diluted ownership hurdle'. They take a couple of big, risky steps that include bringing in non-family managers and sometimes giving up 100% ownership. Three of the companies in *Winning at Services* fit this bill: Securitas, Group 4 Falck and Sodexho.

Bellon explains that his first big hurdle was to employ the first non-family employee. The second big hurdle must have been relinquishing 100% ownership. Bellon, for example, realized early on that if he retained 100% ownership and employed family members only, Sodexho would fall short of industry leadership. In 2001, he passed another big hurdle when he tagged Albert George, a non-family member, to be CEO of Sodexho.

Sørensen of Group 4 Falck has been squeezed through the same emotional wringer as Bellon. Not only did he own the company, but in its heyday, he *was* the company, lock, stock and barrel. Recall from The Journey to Leadership chapter that when the young Sørensen founded Group 4 and started rummaging around for customers, his first customer quickly saw that he was the salesman, the general manager and the security guard. Sørensen and his wife, who later joined Group 4, had no other family members at the time. They had no choice but to hire non-family members or remain small and local. As the company prospered with non-family members supporting its growth, Sørensen retained 100% ownership of Group 4 for 35 years, until, in 2000, he took the wrenching decision to merge Group 4 with Falck, which was quoted on the Copenhagen Stock Exchange. Sørensen became Group 4 Falck's largest shareholder with 37.5%. For 35 years he had been a hands-on chairman and CEO of a 100% family-owned company; now he became a non-executive chairman of a partly family-owned (Sørensen now owns 19.5%) publicly-quoted company with a strong CEO, Nørby Johansen, running daily operations. Did he have the comfort of seeing his children helping manage the new company? No. And yet, under Sørensen's wing, the company has thrived.

Bellon and Sørensen are tough, passionate but unsentimental decision-makers – a different sort: models of owner-managers willing to call the necessary shots to become global leaders of their industries. Likely, without these gutsy moves, the two companies might well have remained mired in mediocrity. The vast majority of family business owners probably don't share Bellon's and Sørensen's ambitions. Fine, but of those who do, only a few are able and willing to take the tough emotional decisions that industry leadership demands. The ability to do what's right for the business first, uncompromising – this is what sets them apart. Berglund, Mackay and Nørby Johansen, though not running family businesses, do the same. They put the needs of the company first, and this, of course, is a matter of mindset.

Win with the right outlook

Put people before systems

Scandinavia has fostered large, labour-intensive outsourcing companies: Sweden's Securitas, Denmark's Group 4 Falck and ISS. The United

Kingdom has brought forth Compass Group and Rentokil (with Danish roots). Ecco (now part of Adecco) came up on French soil. Adia, the second half of Adecco, has Swiss roots. Randstad and Vedior, two of the world's leading employment companies, are from The Netherlands. Like Scandinavia, the United States, since the Second World War, has also fostered some of the best labour-intensive outsourcing companies: Aramark, Marriott catering, Saga Food (catering) and Pinkerton, Burns, and Wackenhut (security). There are household names, too: Manpower, Kelly and ServiceMaster. This first category lives off tailor-made, unique services adapted to the needs of local clients. The United States is also home to another category of well-known service companies, McDonald's, Avis, Hertz, Hilton and the like. These players have a relatively high need to produce identical service output from Lapland to Cape Town, Beijing to Miami.

At the turn of the millennium the *labour-intensive* outsourcing companies in the United States appear to have fallen *behind* their European peers, whereas companies in the second group are *far ahead* of their European peers. How, we asked Berglund, does he explain this? 'I believe', he said, 'that the Americans are incredibly good at running systems-driven service businesses. We Europeans seem to be better at running people-driven service businesses.' This apparent difference, we believe, reflects a deep-seated difference in mindset.

Our type of service firm must focus on people, says Thomas Berglund, not systems. Get the right people in place, motivate and keep them there, keep bureaucracy to a minimum and put as much responsibility for management decisions and service delivery as near the customer as you can. The rest will follow. Good people, the companies believe, can perform well without the rigmarole of endless reports and long chains of command.

We have the impression that, if your company sells a standardized product, your managers may be able to drive the organization from the top by putting systems in place to keep the machinery of the firm spinning. You can, if you are McDonald's, for example, compile a handbook for assembling your standardized, 'McDonaldized' burger, with 16 pieces of onion on top, exactly the same in Seoul as in Anchorage. Or, if you are Hertz or Avis, you can compile a manual on how to rent out a car. But in the service businesses we describe it is up to you to decide whether your business is closer to McDonald's or, say, Securitas where every service is tailor-made – unique. In unique labour-intensive services, it is probably less effective to lead with systems. Better, perhaps, is to lead by motivating and inspiring your staff, developing them, creating the right environment for them to make the right decisions, to want to offer whatever the customer needs or wants, without consulting a manual or following a lock-step system.

If you are selling, say, a fairly customized service to a local customer, then your people have to be at the same level as the customer. So you have to have strong managers who can meet the customer's managers and be partners not servants. That takes a more de-centralized concept because you need to raise the level of your managers much more.

Thomas Berglund, CEO, Securitas

Three of our four companies staff their corporate head offices with between 25 and 50 people. Sodexho's number is somewhat higher. Comparable US companies count 1000 people in their corporate offices. How many more manuals and procedures is a head office with 1000 people likely to churn out than one with 25? Imagine. The hunger for management reports grows, it seems, in direct proportion to the size of the head office: the larger the headquarters the more ravenous the appetite. The 'real' difference between Securitas and the large US companies it acquired (Pinkerton and Burns), explains Berglund, is that Securitas is 'people-driven' and the two US companies were 'systems-driven'. The four companies in our book share this stance. To win at service, the four imply, drive your business with people, not systems.

Win with focus and long horizons

There's more to the difference, however. The chairmen of some large, labour-intensive outsourcing companies in the United States suggest that the Europeans are far ahead in their industries because the incentive for US companies to expand abroad is weaker than it is for, say, a Danish or Swedish company. The United States, with its elephantine market, offers a lot of potential for profitable growth for a long time. Also, with a common language, culture, legislation and other convenient socio-economic trappings, US companies operate more easily on home turf than far afield.

Germany has very fine service companies in the outsourcing industry but, like the Americans, few have substantial operations abroad and none is even close to leading the security and food service industries. We see a number of reasons for this. First, the large German labour-intensive outsourcing companies have – in contrast to our four companies – chosen several games they want to play, their offer includes services such as security, cleaning, catering, or more distantly related services. Second, many have chosen to employ relatively low-skilled, low-paid workers and many part-timers, which means that the German concept is not as universally adaptable as, for instance, the Scandinavian one, since it is low on career opportunity, job rotation and chances to advance. A third reason seems to be that the German market – like the US – is 'big enough' for many.

This difference in the markets may go some way toward explaining the difference in mindsets. The sheer size and 'cultural comfort' of the US and, similarly, German markets, may well serve both to germinate the different mindset toward expansion abroad, and also to reinforce the difference. Says Bill Pollard:

> These companies are all coming out of a European environment, and whether it is in the make-up of the people, the genes so to speak . . . but they have, first of all, a global vision, and then obviously an ability to manage a global business – that is another side of the equation.
>
> Bill Pollard, Chairman, ServiceMaster (USA)

ServiceMaster, according to Pollard, took a hard look at the security industry in the United States before Securitas acquired its way onto America's playing fields. But the American service leader was put off by the high prices. The premium Securitas eventually paid, said Pollard, appeared to be very high. Other European companies, added Pollard, pay high prices for US companies, too. Too high, he seems to imply. The European service companies, however, have shown very impressive operational and financial skills, which has given them highly-valued stocks (shares), which they have used as a currency to buy US companies without diluting their own earnings per share (EPS). The US companies, in contrast, are unable to acquire European service companies with their shares. As an example, a European service company whose market value equalled US$0.80 per US dollar of annual sales, acquired a large American service company that was rated at US$0.18 of annual sales on the New York Stock Exchange for a price corresponding to US$0.30 of annual sales. 'A substantial bid premium of 65%', says the chairman of another US service company we talked to. 'A very reasonable price', says our European CEO, who is confident that he can double the profit margin of the acquired company and thereby create a substantial value for his shareholders.

The four European companies in *Winning at Service* simply do not feel that they are paying too much. The difference, again, stems from mindset. The Americans, thinking relatively short-term, with a strong desire to create quick shareholder value, see the high price tag, and assume that returns won't come soon enough to justify the investment. The Europeans, however, think in terms of long-term growth, three to five years at the least. Securitas, for example, nurtures a strategy of buying 'tired market leaders' such as, for instance, Pinkerton, and revitalizing them by doubling or tripling the profit margins and by increasing the level of organic growth to much higher levels. The mindset – the patience to bring the acquired company *and its people* up to speed over a relatively long horizon – enables Securitas management to see the glass half-full.

A focus on people, not systems, opens the European companies to working more productively with unions than their American counterparts. That the Europeans cooperate so fruitfully with unions *both* in Europe and abroad, and most notably in the United States, seems to puzzle the US chairmen. By tradition, companies in the US security industry prefer to employ non-union labour, pay the minimum wage and spend less on training than their European peers. Securitas and Group 4 Falck, in contrast, believe that they share certain goals with the unions, at least 'ideologically': offering fair pay and decent jobs, and showing respect, they believe, leads to employee and customer satisfaction.

Win at golf: play with a full bag

You can play a good round of golf with a 7-iron – one club. This is what some golfers believe. Champions know better: you win consistently with a full bag. Some managers are like 7-iron golfers. They have a basic degree in some management discipline or other: accounting, marketing, engineering, information technology. They launch their careers with work related to their degrees. And many, even as they scale the career ladder to the top rung – CEO – remain biased toward their original academic degree. Unfortunate. Why? Because the accountant who turns into a managerial control freak counting beans behind office doors is unlikely to create a large, world-class company: thin on people skills; too dispassionate; a blinkered view. The CEO who leans too far towards his sales and marketing 'background' may generate a lot of sales – at the cost of profitability. The CEO with a manufacturing or a technology degree may produce the world's best products and gadgets, but customers don't need them, or want them. Such managers are one-club golfers.

Pierre Bellon, Thomas Berglund, Francis Mackay, Lars Nørby Johansen and J. Philip Sørensen, are 'full bag golfers'. Four trained in accounting or economics. Sørensen, the autodidact, picked up everything on his own. They have grounded themselves in *all* the functional disciplines of management: human resources, finance, investor relations, mergers and acquisitions (M&A), sales and marketing, operations, etc. They have mastered the necessary functional disciplines in a very practical way: when they need a skill or expertise to run the business, they pick it up. They have developed a practical intelligence and apply it every day. They know every nook and cranny of the business. They cannot be hoodwinked by anybody. They do not abide nonsense. They do not take incompetence and laziness lightly. But they are not micro-managers or control freaks. They manage by example. They have learned what they know in their companies over the many years they have been around from the very humble starts, where they were close to the ground. By 'ground' we do not mean fairways and greens, but rather the 'ground' of everyday business. None of the five leaders is a keen golfer. But they carry a full 'bag' of management skills, and unlike many golfers, they master all the clubs, from putter to irons to the BIG Bertha driver. And they know which club to swing for each shot.

Win by turning non-core into core

To thrive, a company must have the right top management teams. But it must also have the right owner. That's why many service divisions in large conglomerates don't work – they've got the wrong owners. Service businesses seem to do better when their managers consider them to be a core business. Compass Group, Group 4 Falck, Securitas and Sodexho have gained their leading position by not only competing with tens of thousands small- and medium-sized competitors; they were also pitted against large competitors owned by financially powerful groups. No doubt, people at the very top of the corporate head offices of huge groups such as Grand Metropolitan, Nestlé, Accor, Wagons Lits, Marriott, Trusthouse Forte, Granada, SAS and Veba longed to build world-leading security and catering businesses. How come none of them succeeded? How come they essentially 'surrendered' their companies to our four? In retrospect, the answer seems simple: they may have had the vision but they did not have the right combination of leadership at the heart, focus, passion for people, and the drive to keep things simple to complete the journey to leadership. And because they didn't, they essentially created what Berglund calls tired market leaders, members of large groups, with the potential to be world-beaters, but that seem, as non-core members of a group, to be waning.

A typical characteristic of the companies that Compass Group, Group 4 Falck, Securitas and Sodexho acquire is that they have led a long life as *non-core division* in another group without becoming a world leader. Compass Group itself was, for many years, a non-core division in the Grand Metropolitan Group (Spirits, Hotels and Catering), now named Diageo after it disposed of its non-core businesses. Diageo is today a world leader in spirits with brand names such as Johnnie Walker, Guinness, Smirnoff, J&B, Baileys, Cuervo, Tanqueray and Malibu.

One of Europe's largest catering companies in the 1980s was Eurest. Owned first by Nestlé and Wagons Lits, it was sold to the French Hotel

Group Accor, which in turn sold it to Compass Group. Nestlé, Wagons Lits, and Accor appeared to be perfectly 'logical' owners. After all, a food manufacturer (Nestlé) and hotel groups (Wagon Lits and Accor) must have synergies – one would think – with a catering business. It was, however, only when Accor sold Eurest to Compass Group that Eurest found the 'right owner'. In Compass Group, whose only business is food service and vending, it became a cornerstone. This platform was the Eurest launching pad. Compass Group has acquired a number of non-core businesses from other groups, including Service Partner from SAS, Scandinavian Airlines System, Canteen from the private equity company, KKR, and Sutcliffe from the media and hotel group Granada Plc through a complex financial transaction.

Sodexho has also bought a myriad of non-core divisions from diversified groups. For example, the catering divisions of the two hotel groups, Marriott and Trusthouse Forte. Sodexho walked into the Scandinavian market by acquiring the Partena Group from the Swedish private equity company Industri Kapital. It also acquired the large catering company Wells from ISS in Brazil.

Our two security companies have also acquired non-core divisions from diversified groups. Securitas bought security companies from Ecco and from ADIA, which merged to form Adecco, the world's largest employment group, Raab Karcher Sicherheit from Veba, a huge German conglomerate which has transformed itself into Eon, one of Europe's largest energy companies, and SecuriSystem, Switzerland, from ISS now known as the world's largest facility service group. Falck took its first large strides into the security business with its acquisition of ISS's Danish security company, ISS Securitas, and broke into the Swedish security market by acquiring Partena Security from Sodexho, who had bought it from Industri Kapital.

Can all companies win?

No, but many can.

We were keen to identify a relevant, credible example of a non-service company that had successfully navigated the journey to leadership using

similar practices to the ones we have described in this book. The obvious
choice was Assa Abloy from Sweden, the world's largest lock manufacturer.
The CEO, Carl-Henric Svanberg, worked for Securitas from 1985 to 1994
as an Operations Director. When Berglund was appointed CEO of
Securitas, Svanberg inherited the task of preparing Securitas' lock
business for sale. We asked Svanberg if he, as CEO of a manufacturing
company, could apply the lessons learnt at Securitas:

> *Yes of course I can. As a manufacturer you buy your raw material from the same*
> *suppliers at the same prices as your competitors do. So you must create competitive*
> *advantage in another way. For me 'the other way' is simple. It can only be through*
> *people. Only people can make a difference.*
>
> Carl-Henric Svanberg, CEO, Assa Abloy

Winning in the locks business

Humble beginnings and an ordinary life (1881–1989)

Assa Abloy sprouted from the seeds of two relatively 'humble' but
nevertheless successful companies: Assa and Abloy. Assa was founded in
Sweden in 1881. For many years up to its acquisition by Securitas, the
company was the leading Swedish lock manufacturer. In the 1950s, Assa
acquired Ruko, the leading Danish locks manufacturer. Assa also
established sales subsidiaries in England and the United States. In the
two decades up to the 1970s, Assa, which was also active in general
hardware as well as locks, was a highly profitable company. During the
1970s, however, profitability started to slip, and by the mid-1980s red
figures began appearing in the profit and loss statements. By concentrating
on locks with higher added value, the company reversed the red trend, but
failed to bring about a lasting change in its fortunes.

Abloy was founded in Finland at the beginning of the twentieth century,
although locks had been manufactured in the Abloy subsidiary, Boda, since
1732. Abloy was, for many years, a highly profitable division of the Finnish
engineering group Wartsila (formerly Metra Oyj). In the mid-1980s the
company followed an expansion strategy that was initially quite successful.

Later, however, profit in the new units in the United States and Germany started falling, and as the 1990s neared, the company's problems started to accelerate.

The turning point (1989)

In 1989, 108 years after Assa's founding, Securitas acquired what was still Sweden's leading – though somewhat battered – lock maker. At the time, Securitas was active only in Sweden, and the general idea behind the acquisition was to broaden the security offer of guards and alarms with locks as well. At the time of the acquisition, Assa had sales of approximately Sw. kr. 400 million and was still losing money. To improve efficiency, the new management crafted a new strategic orientation – with moderately positive results. But a sharp downturn in the Swedish economy merely fuelled Assa's decline. It was time for radical surgery. The number of employees was slashed; volumes suffered; but at the same time, profits ballooned from red to a double digit pretax margin.

Pick your game (1989–1994)

Carl-Henric Svanberg came to Securitas 1985 as president of the alarm division, about the same time as Thomas Berglund. In 1989, Securitas promoted Svanberg and Berglund to executive vice presidents, with Svanberg carrying responsibility not only for all alarm operations but also for the Assa Group. His brief was simple and clear: prepare for the next expansion step or even, perhaps, for disposal.

The challenge, however, was anything but a stroll. At the time, both Assa and Abloy were leading regional players in the Nordic countries in a globally fragmented market. They were local leaders in each market, but basically no one had international ambitions. Assa employed 1000 people, had sales of €45 million and was bleeding money. Not an ideal starting point by any stretch of the imagination.

But Svanberg soon realized that the lock market was as fragmented as the security market – potential for growth was abundant. Deficiencies riddled the company's manufacturing operations, and fixing them looked like a sure source of gain. So, Svanberg developed a vision: to create the world's leading lock manufacturer – a gargantuan challenge. To get Assa ready, Svanberg needed, first and foremost, to turn the group into a profit-spinner. Only then could he find a path forward. It was at this point that the idea of a merger with Abloy came to Svanberg: a merger looked like the perfect opportunity. Svanberg began to turn the idea in his mind. But he didn't act quite yet.

In the meantime, he worked to bring Assa up to speed. Although Assa was a manufacturing company, the pillars of company strategy mirrored those of Securitas: step-by-step development; operational excellence before expansion; focus on core activities, including the divestiture of non-core activities; focus on work flows and work procedures; break down into smaller profit centres; delegate responsibility as far as possible; and reduce staff functions to a minimum. Benchmarking with the more profitable Danish company Ruko also proved very successful. During these years of turning Assa around, Svanberg and his team laid the foundation for the profound understanding of the locks business that would later enable the company to expand rapidly through a series of bold, global acquisitions.

Internationalization (1994–1996)

The merger between Assa and Abloy was consummated in 1994, a turning point in the history of the two firms. Assa had been doing well and aimed to grow. Concurrently, it was becoming apparent to Securitas that the locks business and the guards and alarm business had fewer overlaps and offered fewer synergies than management had anticipated. Assa was manufacturing hardware, selling to installers – in other words, locksmiths – while Securitas was a guarding company that also installed alarms. Both companies had started to expand internationally, and it seemed to make little sense to try to coordinate these activities.

Abloy's problems in the foreign subsidiaries were accelerating. Management needed a boost. The owner, Wartsila, was going through a process of focusing on lesser core activities. So now, suddenly, the old idea of a merger between Assa and Abloy came up again. The time had come. Both groups would add strong brands and strong companies, and if the combined lock-maker could handle the more than ample challenges, there were opportunities galore.

The Initial Public Offering (IPO) was engineered by spinning Assa out to its shareholders, followed by a listing. Immediately thereafter the now three-times-larger Abloy was acquired through a directed issue to Abloy's owner Wartsila. A management team was formed from the managers of the larger units – Sweden, Finland, Norway, Denmark, Germany and the United States – and represented a good balance between the two groups.

The first important step was to divest Card Key, which, with sales of US$60 million, was making heavy losses outside the merged group's core area. This excision bolstered the Assa Abloy earnings and balance sheet; now the combined company could make its first major international acquisition: Essex in the United States. Considering its size and new overseas market, the Essex acquisition, which represented a 60% expansion, was a bit of cliff-walking for Assa Abloy, but it was, nonetheless, critical for continuation. It was, in fact, so important that the *entire* management team got involved in the due diligence. They sketched out myriad scenarios, and ultimately the decision to proceed came by consensus. This procedure – total management involvement right up to consensus – survived, and has since become routine operating procedure for the ensuing acquisition of around 100 companies. Since the first foray into foreign fields, the Essex purchase, Assa Abloy sales have grown eight times, and profits have rocketed upward by a factor of 25.

Industry shaping acquisitions (1996–2002)

Following the US acquisition, Assa Abloy took a giant stride into southern Europe: it acquired the leading French lock group, Vachette, with 2000 employees. Shouldering this large new culture was another big bet that paid off. The company added some more companies in low-cost countries: Fab in the Czech Republic, Urbis in Romania and Scovil in Mexico, each with 1000 employees. These companies were, in Svanberg's words, 'in interesting local markets with long-term potential that also offered the availability of low-cost production of standard products and components'. Growing ever bolder, and more successful, Assa Abloy then added the world leaders in electromechanical locks – effeff in Germany and Securitron in United States with a total of 1200 employees.

In the year 2000, Assa Abloy acquired the global group, Yale. By the turn of the millennium, the firm had added 25 companies with 12 000 employees around the world. Assa Abloy had vaulted into the lead in its industry. Assa Abloy soon added HID, the world leader in identification through cards and readers for access control, and Besam, the world leader in door automatics. Assa Abloy could now offer complete, intelligent door-opening and closing concepts. As of 2002, the firm was a global group by any definition, with 'the necessary competencies to take on true global leadership, not just being the largest but also leading in creativity and thought'.

As with the four service leaders, through this whole evolution the relationship with unions, according to Svanberg, has been great, in spite of rationalizations and sporadic lay-offs. This is no mystery, for Assa Abloy has given considerable time to making sure that unions and employees are well informed and can participate in the company's ongoing discussion of strategy. Local unions often have a healthy long-term view of the company's development. They know that they often survive the present management, and understand that a successful company is the best pledge for the future.

Assa Abloy: Lessons from a non-service winner

What does the Assa Abloy journey to leadership teach us? How are these lessons like the ones learned from Securitas, Group 4 Falck, Compass and Sodexho? As Carl-Henric Svanberg, who learned his 'leadership lessons' at Securitas, says, 'We have a lot in common with Securitas, especially the attitude to people, knowing your job and your numbers, the overarching ambition to simplify so everybody can understand, and the desire to stick to the core.' In more detail:

- *Present the strategy in a few distinct and catchy statements and pictures* that are repeated over and over again (and had better be right!).
- Managers must know their job and make a contribution, for they are selected not for what they have done but for what they *will do* – that is, keep the perspective but never fear the details.
- *Know your numbers* – a handful of key numbers – and your processes.
- *Lead by example*: people will do what you *do*, not what you say.
- *Believe in the employee.* Everyone comes to work with an ambition to do a great job. Win over the employees with the idea and focus their ambition on the vision.
- *Educate the market* – always in security – if you don't see the risk you don't see the need.
- *Synergies often take longer to develop than expected*, while stand-alone earnings can often be more quickly improved than initially assumed.
- *Hold back on focusing synergies until self-confidence and pride grow in the acquired company.*
- Remember that the acquirer often has as much to *learn from the acquired company and vice versa.*

Svanberg's years at Assa Abloy have taught him that 'creating a global leader in locking solutions is based on a three-step strategy'.

> First, create a global platform through the acquisition of locally strong companies, with strong local brands and product programmes, add areas of expertise. Second, develop group strength through joint R&D for leading technologies, centres of excellence for global products and joint production of strategic components. And third, accelerate organic growth through utilizing the global network.
>
> Carl-Henrik Svanberg, CEO, Assa Abloy

How large can winners be?

Service companies probably can't grow for ever, and probably not in the ordinary sense of growth. Our companies typically have grown from, say, 5000 to 200 000 to 300 000 employees over relatively few years. They are all in the Top 20 of Europe's largest employers. Can this continue for ever?

Nothing is linear, nothing goes on for ever – not even the growth of our four companies. None of the five leaders has given us a maximum number of employees that they see as a limit on their payrolls. But there is a limit. Where is it?

Asked this question, Bill Pollard, CEO of ServiceMaster, quoted an answer he got from a very wise man:

> *Bill, when you can no longer identify the size of your company as a benefit to your customers, your company has become too big.*
>
> *Peter Drucker*

Needless to say, we agree with Peter Drucker's eloquent analysis, and so do our four companies. Securitas has identified a growth concept that allows it to grow its 'core' for a very long time while it spins off non-core companies along the way. In its striving to become a pure player, it has sold its cleaning activities. It has spun off Assa Abloy and TelelarmCare to its shareholders. All three disposals trimmed the Securitas group. Several financial analysts believe that Securitas will keep spinning off businesses, and they believe that not only will these businesses sit better with different owners, but that Securitas will become a purer and purer security service player. More specifically, analysts suspect that Securitas will, at the right time, spin off its CIT (cash-in-transit) business and Securitas Direct, its private home alarm business. The spin-off concept was not part of Securitas' initial vision; it emerged while Securitas was on its journey to leadership. The idea is that, after a spin off, the remaining core is 'purer', less complex to manage. Spinning off the superfluous businesses keeps Securitas 'pure' enough to manage it simply and easily. Managers who go with the spin offs, can, like Svanberg of Assa Abloy, become CEOs of a business that can embark on its own journey to leadership.

Does the success of our four service companies and Assa Abloy imply that any company or organization can achieve world leadership by embarking on the journey to leadership? No, of course not. But we do think that every company can learn something that will help them achieve their goal, provided they have one – or, may we suggest, get one. Not necessarily to become world leader, but to become something greater than they are now. Early in the book we said that our leaders seem to go by the mantra, 'If you can dream it, you can make it.' We believe you can too, but only if you and your people have picked your game carefully, put leadership at the heart of the company, have a deep and abiding passion for people, keep everything simple, and, not least, if you and your team have the massive will it takes to stay on course. We believe that the lessons of this book will not go out of fashion, because the lessons from our five leaders will always be relevant to managers who believe that 'it all comes down to people', and it is therefore both simple and complex.

Appendix
Questionnaire for Interviews with CEOs/Chairmen

Company timeline

Before you joined the company
- What happened in the industry?
- What happened in the company?

Snapshot 19xx, the year you joined the company
- How would you describe the state of the industry?
- How would you describe the state of the company?

From when you joined until today
- Why did you become the CEO in 19xx?
- When you arrived, did you have a dream? Did you have a vision? Please describe.
- Did you have a formal business plan with vision, mission, values, strategies, goals, etc.? Describe it.
- Did you set out to become number 1 in the world?
- Who were the key players that executed the plan?
- What was your own role initially?
- What have been your three to five key management challenges as a CEO of the company? Describe these challenges, your actions and the results.
- Looking back, have you missed any significant opportunities?

- Can you think of any mistakes or failures? If so, what have you learnt from them?
- Looking at the timeline and the decisions you took, what moments had the greatest impact on the success of the company?

Why do you think European service companies have become world leaders in several labour-intensive service industries such as yours?

- Have the high wages in Europe helped or hindered? Explain.
- Was it despite or because of European Union (EU) regulations, national labour laws, unions, co-determination, EWC that you as a European company have become number 1 or number 2 in the world?

The next 10 years

- What are your dreams and ambitions for your industry over the next 5–10 years? Describe the industry, as you would like it to look in 2010.

Company details

Business environment

- Who are your customers? How many do you have? Describe your typical customer.
- How do you capture market trends and changes in customer requirements?
- Who are your main competitors? How are you different from your competitors?
- How would you describe your employees?
- What is your role in the industry? Can you give some examples of how you have influenced the standards in the industry?
- To what extent do you work with the unions? You have invited them to one of your high-level management meetings. Why? And with what effect?
- To what extent do investors and financial analysts influence your company's strategy?
- Will you be able to grow faster than the industry average? Explain.
- What do you think about shareholder value versus stakeholder value?
- Have any non-government organizations (NGOs) taken an interest in your company? Examples? Why?

Strategy

- What is the company vision?
- What is the company business model? Who invented the model?
- How do you communicate the model to your employees?

People management

- How do you communicate to your employees? Can you illustrate employee understanding of your vision with an example?
- How do you share best practices across countries? Is everything prescribed in manuals? Explain.
- What is your thinking with regard to recruiting, retaining, developing and rewarding employees? How are your company systems different from those of your competitors?

Leadership

- What three to five leadership characteristics enable people to succeed in your company?
- How is this different from your competitors and those in other industries?
- How do you select leaders? Describe in detail.
- How do you reward success? Describe in detail.
- What kind of incentives do you have in your company? Describe in detail.
- How much (%) of the company is owned by management and employees?
- How do you train and develop managers? How is group management involved in training? How are you personally involved? Do you have a corporate university? What percentage of turnover is spent on training?

Head office

- What does your head office do? What functions do you keep in the head office, and which ones do you keep out in the divisions and countries? How many people do you have in the head office? How do you see the role of your head office?
- Do you use management consultants to develop your strategies or other areas of the business? Explain.

The role of the CEO/Chairman of the company

Your role

- How do you see your role in the company?
- What do you focus on? Why?

- How do you spend your time?
- Where do you get your inspiration?
- What are your major contributions to the success of the company?
- What is on your mind right now to secure that your company will remain a world leader?

Your life before you started working for the company
- What was your family situation?
- How did you experience school?
- What were you good at?
- What were you bad at?
- What have been the main challenges in your life?
- What was your first leadership position?

Miscellaneous
- What do you consider your most important contribution to the success of the company?
- What, in your view, are the real secrets behind the success of the company?
- What *simple* advice would you have for managers?
- If you were writing a book like ours, what would you say were the key ingredients to your success? And how would you present them to managers in a book? In other words, how or what can other senior executives learn from your story?

Wrap-up

- To find out why your company became this successful, who else should we talk to?
- Have we missed out anything you think should be said?

Miscellaneous

Each CEO/Chairman research interview included 5–10 company specific questions designed to elicit further explanations about the company.

Index